N I C K F

Heart to Heart

Reflective thoughts and prayers

kevin
mayhew

First published in 2004 by
KEVIN MAYHEW LTD
Buxhall, Stowmarket, Suffolk, IP14 3BW
E-mail: info@kevinmayhewltd.com

9 8 7 6 5 4 3 2 1 0

ISBN 1 84417 319 4
Catalogue No. 1500734

Cover design by Angela Selfe
Edited and typeset by Katherine Laidler

Printed and bound in Great Britain

Contents

Introduction

Is there a right way to pray? As I understand it, definitely not. There is no set pattern or form of words we have to use, still less any religious language in which prayer should be couched. What works for one leaves another cold, so much depending on people's background, character, tradition and, above all, their understanding and experience of God. The one essential, as far as I'm concerned, is that prayer comes from the heart, honestly expressing what we want to say to God. Some find that the only way to do this is through extemporising their own prayers; others find this well-nigh impossible, needing written prayers to help articulate their own thoughts and feelings. Most fall somewhere in the middle, quite happy to pray privately and personally, but finding written prayers a helpful stimulus.

This book aims to provide such a stimulus, offering 75 reflective prayers exploring the nature and journey of Christian discipleship. Drawn from several of my study books published over recent years, each is prefaced by a brief passage of Scripture followed by a short introduction, both designed to set the context of the prayer itself. The prayers are conversational in tone, deliberately so, reflecting the fact that God invites us to open our hearts to him as a friend, in the knowledge that his heart is open to us in turn. Whether in personal devotion or public worship, it is my hope that this book will help to prompt further reflection and to express our ongoing relationship with God in Christ.

NICK FAWCETT

Introduction

CELEBRATING LIFE

1
This is the day

This is the day that the Lord has made; let us celebrate and exult in it. Psalm 118:24

One of the truths we can lose sight of sometimes, even as Christians, is that God wants us to enjoy life. We can forget that for all kinds of reasons: perhaps due to pressures of work or other demands; perhaps illness affecting us or loved ones; perhaps worry about the future or regrets over the past; and so we could go on. In time, we get sucked along by life, no longer pausing to count our blessings as we once did. As Christians, we perhaps should be different, but the reality is that we can be more guilty than any, turning the life of faith into a duty rather than spontaneous celebration. Yet throughout Scripture we find a repeated emphasis on the joy, blessing and fulfilment God longs to give his people, not just in some future heavenly kingdom but also here and now. Yes, the gospel involves demands and responsibilities, and, yes, life brings its fair share of trials and tragedy, but the message at the heart of our faith is that, come what may, God is with us, his love continuing through all. That, surely, is good news to celebrate!

Pray

I'd lost sight of what it is all about, Lord,
  of your gift at the heart of the gospel –
  a joy beyond words,
  bubbling up within me,
  brimful,
  overflowing.

I brooded instead on faults and failings,
worrying about the weakness of my love,
wrestling with matters of doctrine,
and fretting over the cost of discipleship,
forgetting that though these are all part of commitment,
they are not the whole,
and not finally what matters most.
But then you spoke again,
reminding me that you accept me as I am,
your love not earned but given;
emphasising that though I repeatedly let you down,
still you stay faithful,
nothing able to exhaust your grace.
The old self lives on,
yet I realise afresh
that you are constantly making all things new,
offering life in abundance,
now and for all eternity.
Gracious God,
I pause,
I reflect,
I remember the wonder of your love,
and so once more I celebrate
with heart and mind and soul.
This day, like all days, is your gift:
I will rejoice and be glad in it.
Amen.

2
Living life to the full

I have come so that you might have life, and live it to the full.
John 10:10b

Life lived to the full – is that what distinguishes us as Christians? I'd like to think so, but it's by no means always the case. All too easily we can substitute the abundant life Jesus offers for a pale imitation, confusing faith with religion and discipleship with church. Some get sucked into church life to the point that there's little room for anything else. Others draw away from the world, shutting out what they see as pagan influences that might lead them or their families astray. Others again wash their hands of this life in a different sense, claiming that we should not concern ourselves with social and environmental issues but focus instead on life to come. Is this 'life in all its fullness'? Not for me, it isn't! I can understand where such people are coming from, but to me these attitudes seem a denial rather than affirmation of life. Of course, not everything in this world is good, so, yes, we do need to exercise discernment and know where to draw the line, but we need also to recognise the good in life – the special and beautiful, everything that has the capacity to fascinate, inspire, challenge, thrill and bless – recognising and receiving it as God's gift.

Pray

It sounds so wonderful, Lord,
so rich and replete with promise:
life in all its fullness –
abundant,
overflowing.

But do I live in such a way as to show that,
in a way that makes people sit up and take notice,
desiring such life for themselves?
Is each day a celebration of your goodness,
each moment a joyful response
to the blessings you so freely bestow?
Or do people see in me instead a denial of life,
taking refuge in creed and doctrine, religion and ritual,
retreating into the safe environment
of church and fellowship,
rather than embracing all that is good in your world,
the inestimable treasures it has to offer?
It's not easy striking the right balance,
for neither life nor this world are all good –
not by a long way –
so much bringing pain and sorrow,
so much tarnished by evil,
spoiled by sin.
Yet life is still your gift,
fashioned by your hand and bearing your stamp;
a bequest to be savoured,
sanctified,
celebrated.
Teach me, then, Lord, to live within this world
yet not be conformed to it,
to affirm the best and challenge the worst,
living each day,
each moment,
in joyful thanksgiving.
Teach me to anticipate your promise of life to come
by consecrating life *now*
and living it to your praise and glory.
In Christ's name I pray.
Amen.

3
One day at a time

So do not brood about tomorrow; you can be sure it will bring its sufficient share of difficulties. Take one day at a time, for each has enough problems of its own. Matthew 6:34

How much of our lives, I wonder, do we waste worrying about some eventuality that ultimately never transpires? Few things are more destructive than worry, yet few things harder to overcome. We turn over a host of possibilities in our minds, wondering how we might cope if such and such comes about, when most of the time our anxiety is misplaced, things working out very differently. As a result, we end up looking back ruefully, regretting the happiness and peace of mind we could have enjoyed if only we had been able to put our unease to one side. Can we learn to do so? Well, we can make a start by keeping in mind the salutary words of Jesus, 'Which of us by worrying can add even a fraction to our height?' Far from changing anything, worry actually wears us out, lessening our ability to cope if what we dread finally happens. Instead of fretting over the past, brooding about what tomorrow might hold, we need to learn to take one day at a time, celebrating it for what it is, and trusting God to see us through whatever the future might hold.

Pray

'Take things as they come,' you say.
'One day, one moment, at a time.'
And I know it makes sense, Lord;
  that it's foolish to fret,
  for what's done is done
  and what must be will be.

Yet I can't help dwelling sometimes on the past
and brooding on the future:
the things I should have done
and those I *have* done;
the things I hope will come
and those that *might* come.
I saw the man rushed to hospital
and I thought that one day it could be me.
I saw the patient in the nursing home
and I feared one day it *will* be me.
I saw the baby in the photo
and I reflected that one day, not so long ago,
it *was* me.
Times gone by,
times to come,
and both scare me in their way,
for one's over,
lost for ever,
and the other lies in wait,
no knowing what it might bring,
for good or ill.
But I know one thing, Lord;
remind me of that:
the truth that your love endures for ever,
the same yesterday, today and tomorrow.
Teach me, then, that whatever life may bring,
you will be with me in it,
there by my side to strengthen,
sustain,
succour
and support.
In that knowledge may I put all in your hands,
and live each moment as your gift
in grateful praise
and joyful service.
Amen.

COMFORT IN SORROW

4
The God of all comfort

Blessed are those who mourn, for they will receive comfort.
Matthew 5:4

Is there any blessing in sorrow? It's hard to think so, isn't it? The very thought of tragedy sends a chill up our spines, causing us to push it to the back of our minds, and it's natural we should feel that way, for God doesn't want us to idealise grief or unhappiness. Yet life, inevitably, will bring its share of heartache, and, however hard that will be to bear, we have the promise of his comfort to support us and see us through.

Pray

I don't know how I'll cope, Lord,
  I really don't.
When tragedy strikes,
  as one day it unquestionably will,
  I'm not sure how I'll take it;
  whether I'll have the strength I need,
  the inner resources,
  to keep my head above water,
  or whether I'll sink like a stone,
  overwhelmed by the trauma,
  engulfed by grief,
  drowning in despair.
I hope I'll be strong,
  but even the *thought* of calamity sets my hairs on end,
  never mind the reality.
I dread the aching sense of loss,
  the pall of sorrow,
  the utter brokenness of heart and spirit,

those themselves too much to bear,
but I fear also
the simplistic words of consolation some will offer,
sincere enough,
well-intended,
yet promising peace where there is no peace,
cheer where there is no cheer
and answers where there is only confusion.
Remind me, Lord, of your assurance
that those who mourn shall be comforted,
that tears will give way to laughter
and light triumph over darkness.
Remind me that whatever I face, I will not be alone;
that in the shadow of sorrow
and the valley of death
you will be there.
And remind me, also, of all those across the years
who have discovered the same,
finding in you not just one to share their pain
but one also who leads them through it
to new beginnings,
a new dawn.
Would I cope, Lord?
I just don't know,
but thankfully even if *I* fail,
you won't,
your love unfailing,
your promise true,
your comfort assured.
Receive my praise,
in Jesus' name.
Amen.

5
God in the darkness

Rejoice in the Lord constantly; I repeat: rejoice constantly.
Philippians 4:4

Anyone who has suffered the pain of tragedy will know that grief doesn't go away quickly; indeed, the wounds sometimes never fully heal. To those enduring heartbreak it can seem as though a light has been extinguished, never to shine again. How, then, can Paul exhort us to rejoice constantly? The very idea seems absurd. And indeed it would be if he meant by this that people should be cheerful every moment of every day. What he had in mind, though, I think, was something very different: an ability to rejoice even in times of sorrow due to a conviction that God is present even there. There is no quick fix to sadness, but at the heart of our faith is the conviction that God shares even the darkest moments with us and will ultimately lead us through.

Pray

'Rejoice in the Lord always' –
  isn't that what we're told to do?
'Give thanks in all circumstances.'
'Make music in your hearts.'
And that's what I've done, Lord –
  most of the time, anyway –
  life being good to me,
  with so much to celebrate,
  so many reasons to give you thanks.
But now it's different,
  for I've come face to face with sorrow,
  grief no longer being about others but about me.

I've felt the agony of loss,
the pain of separation,
and where flowers once bloomed
life has become a desert.
I've tasted the gall of loneliness,
the bitterness of tears,
and where wine once flowed
now there is only vinegar.
It's been hard to praise you through that, Lord,
to sing a new song,
to make a joyful noise,
for I've been heavy within,
the sparkle gone not just from life but from faith.
Yet even there, in the darkness, I have glimpsed your face,
your hand leading me through,
and I realise now, as light beckons once more,
that you were there with me all along,
as you are with me always,
bearing my sorrow,
sharing my pain,
not expecting me to laugh through the tears
but gently wiping them away,
easing the hurt and bandaging up my wounds.
Lord, for your faithfulness even in the darkest moments,
your love that will not let me go,
receive my glad thanksgiving,
in the name of Christ.
Amen.

6
Rescue us from evil

Rescue us from evil. Matthew 6:13b

What does it mean to pray, 'Rescue us from evil'? Can prayer ever inoculate us against suffering and sorrow, heartache and hardship? The answer, of course, is no. Misfortune, suffering and hardship afflict the Christian as much as anyone else, and anyone who thinks otherwise is sadly deluded. God does not wish such things upon us, but they are an inescapable facet of being human. What Jesus meant when he urged his followers to use these words was that we should seek God's help in every situation to overcome whatever might separate us from him or cause us to lose faith. Such pressures and temptations are more powerful than we might imagine, and, however committed we believe ourselves to be, none of us, by our own efforts, can be confident of not falling. We need God's strength and support to see us through.

Pray

'Lord, save me!' I cried.
'Protect me!'
'Deliver me!'
But disaster struck nonetheless,
    bringing heartbreak,
    hurt,
    confusion.
'Lord, bring healing!' I begged.
'Bring wholeness!'
'Make well!'

But there was no happy ending,
no sudden and miraculous recovery –
just the harrowing and lingering death
of one I loved.
And I threw up my hands in anger,
asking 'Why?'
'How?'
'Where was God when I needed him?'
It shook me to the core,
my faith buckling,
all but broken,
until I remembered that those words,
'rescue us from evil',
were spoken by your Son
who went on to face evil at its fiercest,
suffering and sorrow as great as anyone's,
and I realised that the brokenness of this world
grieves you as much as me.
You were there all along, sharing the hurt,
weeping over everything that denies your love
and frustrates your purpose,
but you were there also to support and strengthen,
reaching through the pain to share it and bear it,
and finally to lead us through.
Remind me of that whenever life is hard
and days are dark,
and teach me, then above all times,
to pray from the heart:
'rescue me from evil'.
Amen.

COSTLY DISCIPLESHIP

See also FAITH IN ACTION

7
A hostile response

You will encounter hatred and hostility because of your commitment to me, but whoever keeps faith to the end will be saved. Matthew 10:22

How many of us would stay true to our faith if it were to prove costly, even dangerous? Thankfully, we are unlikely to be put to that test, but there may nonetheless come times when Christian commitment involves making a stand for what we believe in that might prove unpopular with some and that might ask of us more courage than we'd like to be asked of us. How would we respond in such a time?

Pray

Lord,
   I don't like trouble –
   in fact it terrifies me,
   the very thought sending shivers down my spine –
   so I steer well clear,
   avoiding controversy,
   keeping my head down,
   restricting my faith, as far as possible,
   to something between me and you,
   no one else.
Yet, in my heart, I know that will not do,
   for there have been times –
   far too many –
   when I should have stood firm,
   stuck my neck on the line,
   but failed to do so.
I saw injustice

and kept quiet,
witnessed evil
and looked the other way,
each time claiming it wasn't my business,
not my job to get involved.
But it *was*,
for if *I* ignore it *others* will do the same,
and what's done to one today
will be done to many tomorrow,
perhaps even to me.
Teach me, Lord, when necessary, to risk conflict,
even hostility,
for the sake of truth;
to endure resentment,
unpopularity,
for the sake of right;
to face hardship,
even danger,
for the sake of good.
Teach me to stand up for you,
ready to risk some cost
for you who paid the ultimate price.
Amen.

8
Divided loyalties

It is impossible to serve two masters . . . You cannot simultaneously serve God and the world. Matthew 6:24

Christian discipleship, if it is authentic, will almost certainly lead, at times, to a conflict of interests, times when we are faced by a straight choice between a demanding way that we know to be right and an easier way that we know to be wrong. How will we react on such occasions? It's tempting to try to play it both ways, steer a middle course that gives us the best of both worlds, but, as the words of Jesus make clear, in attempting to have a foot in both camps we may end up without having one in either.

Pray

I thought I'd decided, Lord,
committed myself irrevocably to your service,
without reserve or qualification,
but I see now I was wrong.
When faith involved sacrifice,
putting *you* first and *self* second,
I realised I was hedging my bets,
serving you when it suited
but determined to serve my own ends also.
I imagined I could marry the two,
stay faithful to you yet leave space for me,
and I was right, some of the time,
for there was no clash of interests,
no reason not to savour the joys of this world
alongside the blessings of heaven.

But occasionally it was different,
your call involving choices –
stark,
demanding,
costly;
the challenge to give and go on giving,
to say no to compromise,
to stand up for justice, against the odds,
to speak out for faith where few would listen –
choices I'd rather not make,
challenges I'd no wish to face.
So I tried steering a middle course,
a path between the two,
only to find I achieved nothing,
pleasing neither you nor me.
Forgive me,
and help me to decide where my priorities lie.
Teach me to put you first, above all else,
renouncing whatever may keep me from your side
or prevent me from following your way.
Whenever choices must be made,
Lord, help me to make them,
staying faithful to you, come what may.
Amen.

9
Beyond the call of duty

Do not resist an evildoer, but if someone strikes you on the right cheek, offer the other cheek too. If anyone decides to sue you and take your coat, let them have your cloak as well, and whoever forces you to go one mile, go with them a second also.
Matthew 5:39-41

How much are you ready to do for others? How much are you prepared to offer to God? Many of us, if we're honest, are guilty sometimes of giving as little as we can, preferring to look after number one before considering anyone else. The idea of going the extra mile – giving not only what's expected of us but more besides – doesn't come any easier to us than it did to the Jews of Jesus' day, but that's what's involved in true Christian discipleship: gladly, freely and spontaneously doing that little bit extra – and doing so not simply because we *must* but, above all, because we *may*.

Pray

'Do I have to?' I thought.
'Can't they see I'm busy?'
Yes, I know it's a good cause,
  and of course I'd like to support it –
  in an ideal world,
  where time's no object,
  money no problem.
But it's not like that, is it!
There's the mortgage to pay,
  food to put on the table,
  children to get ready for school;
  there's the lawn to cut,
  washing and ironing to see to,

jobs needing doing around the house –
these and so much else,
and I need two pairs of hands just to get those done,
let alone anything more.
Make time for others?
Give to the needy?
I'd love to, truly,
but there's only so much anyone can do,
and it seems to me I'm doing it already.
Is that how I argue, Lord?
I hope not,
and I doubt I'd be quite so blunt,
quite so grudging,
yet, truth be told,
beneath the good intentions,
the pious veneer,
that's the way my mind works sometimes –
more often than I care to admit.
Instead of how *much* I can do, it's how *little.*
Instead of what I can offer, it's what I can keep back.
Instead of giving extra, it's cutting down
on the fraction I occasionally give.
Forgive me, Lord,
for I don't just impoverish others
through such meanness of spirit,
but also myself.
Teach me to follow Christ,
who gave not just a proportion extra
but everything.
May I learn from him that in letting go of self
I gain hold of life abundant;
that in giving I receive,
and that in responding to others
I respond above all to you.
In his name I ask it.
Amen.

10
The courage of our convictions

Blessed are those who are persecuted for the sake of right; to them belongs the kingdom of heaven. Exult and celebrate, for you will be richly recompensed in heaven; in similar fashion they victimised the prophets before you. Matthew 5:10, 12

Few Christians today, in the Western world at least, are persecuted for their faith. We are free to worship and believe as we will, and to express ourselves, within reason, as we see fit. Any hostility we are likely to suffer is negligible. Yet ironically, despite so little being asked of us, we are probably less prepared than any generation before us to risk even the outside chance of embarrassment, misunderstanding or ridicule for the sake of the gospel, preferring to keep our discipleship under wraps rather than lose credibility or face an adverse response. That's fully understandable, of course, for no one in their right mind welcomes persecution, but there may be times when true commitment turns out also to be *costly* commitment, any other way being no commitment at all.

Pray

Lord,
  I'm not persecuted –
  not for my faith, my convictions or anything else.
I'm able to worship you as I will,
  believe what I will
  and decide as I will –
  free to live according to my own conscience
  rather than as anyone might dictate –
  and for all that I give you my heartfelt thanks.
You offer each day as a gift to be celebrated,
  wanting us all to rejoice in life, without fear or reserve,

yet don't let me hide behind that,
avoiding the sacrifices
that faithful discipleship might entail,
for if others are to enjoy the same gift in turn,
it may occasionally mean facing antagonism,
adversity,
even affliction
to safeguard that heritage.
If I need to make a stand,
however unpopular,
give me courage to make it.
If I need to speak out against evil,
even though it might cost me friendship,
give me integrity to do so.
If I need to talk of your kingdom, your love, your purpose,
even though others may ridicule
or misinterpret what I say,
give me courage to continue nonetheless.
Whatever it might mean to be persecuted
for the sake of right,
should you ask me to pay that price
enable me to honour your call.
Teach me to rejoice in the blessings of life,
but above all to remember
the blessings that go beyond it –
eternal blessings that you alone can give –
and equip me to live in such a way that,
however great the cost,
I may not only make those blessings mine
but also enable others to enjoy them in turn.
Amen.

11
The law of love

Don't let anyone imagine I've come to do away with the law or the prophets. On the contrary, far from doing away with them, I've come to fulfil them. I'm telling you straight, until heaven and earth are no more, not one detail of the law, not even a miniscule point of punctuation, will be discarded unless the whole has been realised. Matthew 5:17-18

Rules, we sometimes say, are made to be broken; in other words, the spirit of the law can, on occasions, be very different to the letter. That, for me, gives us some idea of what Jesus had in mind when he spoke of fulfilling rather than doing away with the Law and the prophets. Accused by the scribes and Pharisees of openly flouting religious taboos and guidelines, Jesus saw things differently, arguing that everything that the Law and prophets stood for could be summed up in one commandment: to love. No longer, he implied, can we take rules off the peg and apply them rigidly come what may. No longer can we set down black-and-white prescriptions concerning the rights and wrongs of every action, each set for ever in stone. Instead of what we *can't* do, true faith emphasises what we *can* do, asking us in each and every situation to consider how we might fulfil God's will through showing his love in action.

Pray

I saw the signs, Lord –
'No parking',
'No entry',
'Keep off the grass',
'Trespassers will be prosecuted' –
and I realised, to my shame, that I see *you* like that:

as someone who sets rules, regulations,
boundaries on my behaviour,
telling me 'Don't do this! Don't do that!' –
setting out what's right and wrong,
acceptable or unacceptable,
all laid out in stark, uncompromising terms.
But that's not what I see in Christ –
nothing like it!
I see instead one who repeatedly pronounced forgiveness,
who mixed with those condemned as sinners,
and who challenged those without sin
to cast the first stone;
the one who emphasised not what we *can't* do
but what we *can*,
summing up the law in terms of a new commandment,
the call to love.
Teach me, Lord, that this is no easy option
or fudging of the issues,
but, if taken seriously, a challenge far deeper,
infinitely more costly and demanding,
but expressing your will
in a way that the letter of the law can never begin to.
Save me from a narrow, bigoted
and self-righteous attitude;
a preoccupation with rules and regulations;
a hiding behind pious moralising
that saves me from facing real issues
for real people
in real situations.
Teach me what it means to live by the law of love,
and, by your grace, help me to do that as best I can,
in every relationship,
every action,
every day,
to the glory of your name.
Amen.

12
Do as you would be done by

In everything do as you would be done by; this encapsulates what the law and the prophets are all about. Matthew 7:12

Do as you would be done by. If only people followed that precept, what a different world it would be. It provides a perfect synopsis of Christian ethics, so apparently straightforward yet having far-reaching consequences. The problem, of course, is that people don't observe it, and because *they* don't we tend to see little reason why *we* should either, but that is to follow *our* way rather than the way of Christ. If there is to be any prospect of change in our world, any possibility of God's kingdom coming a little closer here on earth, then it needs you and me, all who confess the name of Christ, to do what we can, no matter how small, to help make a difference. If *we* don't lead the way, why should anyone follow?

Pray

Nice one, Lord!
You've hit the nail on the head,
  your summary of the law and prophets
  encapsulating all I try to live by:
  doing to others as I've had done to me.
That's right, isn't it?
Of course it is . . .
  what else could you mean?
If someone wrongs me, I'll look to get even,
  naturally –
  it's a question of simple justice.
If someone picks a fight,
  starts a quarrel,
  then they'll get what's coming to them.

All right,
so perhaps occasionally I'm the transgressor –
acting unkindly,
doing what you'd rather I didn't –
but if so there'll be good reason, you can be sure of that,
such behaviour the exception rather than the norm.
It's a matter of give and take, I suppose –
I'll scratch their back if they scratch mine:
that's what you're after, Lord, isn't it?
What's that?
I've got it wrong?
Surely not!
You can't mean do to others what I'd *have* done to me
instead of what I've *had* done!
You *do*, don't you!
You really want me to put others first and self second!
But that's such a huge gamble,
such a massive leap of faith!
And who can say where it all might lead?
I thought I'd understood,
but I hadn't;
I *still* haven't –
my head in a spin as I struggle to take it in,
let alone accept and follow.
I need help, Lord,
your Spirit within me,
for I can't do it alone,
even should I wish to.
Give me the strength I need,
the courage to deal with others your way,
as you say,
recognising that, costly though it may seem,
it is no more so –
indeed, far less –
than the way you have dealt with me in Christ.
Amen.

FAITH AND DOUBT

See also TRUST IN GOD'S FUTURE

13
Searching for enlightenment

If you yearn for understanding with all your heart, and cry out for insight, seeking it as for precious and hidden treasure – then you will grasp what it means to fear God and will comprehend more about him. Proverbs 2:2b-3a, 4-5

I have always been a believer in doubt. That might sound incongruous, many seeing doubt as the antithesis of faith, but, in my book, if God is God, then, in this life at least, there will always be much we do not and *cannot* understand. Such doubt, though, should not be a negative thing, sapping commitment or clouding vision; we don't know everything about all kinds of things, including the people we meet, but that doesn't make our experiences and relationships any less meaningful. Rather, it inspires us to learn more, to uncover new depths, to seek further enlightenment, life a continuing and exciting journey of discovery. The same should be true for us as Christians. There is much that we do not as yet grasp, but, building on what we *do* know, we press on to discover more of truth, more of God's saving and sovereign love.

Pray

Lord,
　there is so much I don't understand,
　so much that, if I'm honest, troubles me:
　questions concerning evil and suffering,
　the nature of truth and authority of Scripture;
　uncertainties about the origins of life
　and our ultimate goal;
　doubts over matters of creed and doctrine,
　even sometimes your very existence.

I don't question lightly, far from it,
for such things strike at the heart of my faith,
threatening everything I believe –
or, at least, everything I'm meant to believe –
yet I can't help it,
for there's no use pretending,
no point claiming everything is all right
when it clearly isn't.
I might fool others,
but not you,
or me,
so where would that get us?
No,
I can only continue searching,
looking for answers for as long as it takes,
trusting that one day, in your own time,
the quest will be over,
the journey complete,
the understanding I seek finally granted.
Until then, Lord,
go with me,
lead me,
teach me.
Show me, as you have promised,
that those who seek *will* find!
Amen.

14
Life's riddle

How long, Lord, shall the wicked prosper, how long will they gloat? Psalm 94:3

There's no getting away from it: in this world, at least, life's not fair. Evil not only goes unpunished but often thrives. Good often goes unrecognised, the weak are trampled over, and the poor are left to fend for themselves. How can we make sense of God in all this? Where does it leave our faith? If questions like those trouble you sometimes, take heart, for they have troubled many before you, finding their way into Scripture itself. The book of Job and many of the minor prophets raise them loud and clear, and they find more than a passing mention also in books like Ecclesiastes and the Psalms. No easy answers are offered – quite simply, there aren't any – but each finally comes to the conclusion that sometime, somehow, God will reveal what lies hidden, his justice finally prevailing.

Pray

Lord,
  try as I might I can't help questioning sometimes,
  can't help wondering why evil seems to prosper
  and good goes unrewarded.
I know that shouldn't matter –
  that there's more to life than money,
  power,
  prestige,
  possessions –
  but occasionally it gets to me nonetheless,

so that I doubt not only your justice
but also whether you're even there at all.
How can you ignore wrongdoing,
overlook so much that flouts your will,
not just turning a blind eye
but allowing evil to flourish
while virtue goes to the wall?
It doesn't make sense –
life sometimes an enigma
and faith a puzzle.
Only that, of course, is seeing things my way,
according to my values,
my yardstick,
confusing worldly wealth with divine blessing,
earthly pleasure with eternal fulfilment.
Forgive me, Lord,
and teach me to trust in your justice,
recognising that you alone can see into the heart
and weigh our lives in the balance.
Teach me, then, to look to myself,
and to leave the verdict on others to you.
In Christ's name I pray.
Amen.

15
Can things really change?

Behold, I make all things new. Revelation 21:5

It's all very well to say that God's purpose will triumph; the question is: how? Does it really make any sense, given the harsh realities of this world, to talk of good defeating evil, hope conquering despair, and love triumphing over hatred? Can we even begin to speak of God's kingdom beginning on earth, as it is in heaven? If such matters rested solely with us, the answer would have to be no. We cannot even change ourselves, let alone the world. But the change that the gospel speaks of depends on God, a God who is constantly working to bring new beginnings. This, of course, is an ongoing process, only finally to be realised in the fullness of time, but it starts now, God able to transform every situation, no matter how hopeless it may seem. We may feel that nothing can change – but what seems impossible to us is possible for God.

Pray

Lord God,
  I used to believe this world could be different –
  that love could overcome hate,
  good conquer evil
  and joy triumph over sorrow –
  but I'm not so sure now.
I do still believe it –
  or, at least, part of me does –
  but not with the same passion and intensity I once felt,
  faith being tinged with doubt,
  hope coloured by despair.

There have been too many disappointments,
too many false dawns,
each promising so much
yet delivering so little.
One tyranny ends,
another begins.
One wrong is righted,
another takes its place.
The faces may be different
but human nature stays depressingly the same,
and it's hard,
so very hard,
to keep faith alive –
to accept that anything can really change.
Lord, remind me of all you did in Christ . . .
and all you continue to do through him.
Speak to me of the lives you have transformed
and of those you are still transforming.
Help me to glimpse again
the wholeness you have brought,
the commitment you've inspired
and the service offered in your name,
each a symbol of your renewing, redeeming love.
Break through the walls of disillusionment
and despondency,
and revive a sense of all you are able to do,
all you *will* do,
and all you are doing *even now,*
through Jesus Christ,
the King of kings and Lord of lords.
Amen.

16
Making sense of it all

I guarantee that I will be with you every day, to the very end of time. Matthew 28:20

If doubt can be a positive thing, it can also be negative, causing faith to collapse and die. If we brood on what we don't know, forgetting what we *do*, if we let bad experiences obscure the good, or if we assume that because *we* can't make sense of something it clearly doesn't make sense at all, we will soon find belief starting to waver, convictions we once held dear crumbling into dust. We need to learn to live with mystery, with the fact that now we see only in part. That's not to encourage blind faith, but to emphasise rather the need for trust based on personal experience. We must look back to the ways God has blessed us, holding on to those times when he has seemed very near, and letting such experiences support us when he feels distant. Above all, we must cling on to God's promise in Christ that he is with us always, now and for all eternity – whether we see him or whether we don't.

Pray

I shouldn't have doubted, Lord, I know that,
  but I couldn't help it,
  for I called and you didn't seem to answer,
  I searched but never seemed to find,
  and all of a sudden you felt distant,
  detached,
  disinterested,
  no longer part of my daily life,
  no longer part of anything.

I kept faith as best I could, believe me,
but each day it was that little bit harder,
conviction starting to crumble and questions to grow
as still you appeared absent –
aloof to my plight,
remote from this world.
But then, piece by piece, the jigsaw came together,
hindsight revealing what was hidden at the time:
that you'd been there all along –
holding,
guiding,
loving,
caring,
supporting me when I stumbled,
carrying me when I fell –
always close by my side.
Thank you, Lord, that whether I see it or whether I don't,
your hand is upon me;
that however remote you may seem,
you are always near –
unrecognised perhaps,
unnoticed,
but unfailing.
In that knowledge, I will put my trust,
this and every day.
Amen.

17
Difficult choices

Come on, I'm giving you a straight choice today between life and death, good and evil. Deuteronomy 30:15

'A straight choice' – if only life were always that simple. It *is* sometimes, of course, when the boundaries between right and wrong are all too apparent, but in so many areas of life we are faced with the need to discriminate between shades of grey rather than black and white. So often there appear to be two equally valid points of view, each with their plus sides and each with their negative. How do we decide between them? Does faith give us a clear-cut answer every time? I don't think so. Instead, we have to make up our own minds, seeking God's guidance certainly, and acting upon it, but ultimately having to make the choice ourselves. Sometimes we can sit on the fence, keeping an open mind for as long as possible. At other times, though, that isn't an option – decisions affecting us or others have to be made, like it or not. As well as needing God's help to find the answers, we need it sometimes simply to face the questions.

Pray

I'm trying to decide, Lord,
believe me, I'm trying,
and if you'd asked me yesterday
I'd have said I'd succeeded,
my mind made up,
the debate over.
Only I couldn't escape that little voice in my head,
refusing to be silenced,
insisting there was more to the matter than I'd allowed.

I tried to ignore it, but it was no good,
for, unfortunately, it was true,
the more I stopped to consider it,
the more complicated I saw the issue was.
There weren't just two sides to the argument but many,
each with their pros and cons,
their good and their bad points,
and instead of leading me towards an answer,
they took me further away,
my head suddenly spinning with uncertainty.
I wish I could go back to how it used to be –
everything straightforward,
cut and dried,
for it was easy that way,
no need to think for myself,
in fact, no real decision to take;
but I realise now that life isn't like that,
not neat and tidy,
not simple or straightforward at all.
I can't say I like it, Lord,
wrestling with choices,
accepting that what I thought was right
may turn out to be wrong,
but if I'm serious about finding answers,
not mine but yours,
then I need first to face the questions,
and to listen to what you are saying to me through them.
Amen.

FAITH IN ACTION

See also COSTLY DISCIPLESHIP

18
Practising what we preach

Not everyone saying to me, 'Lord, Lord' will enter the kingdom of heaven, but only the one who does the will of my heavenly Father. Matthew 7:21

Those words of Jesus are disturbing, aren't they? – so disturbing that some prefer to ignore them. After all, they argue, we're justified by faith, not works, salvation given by God's grace alone. And, of course, they're right, for God accepts us as we are, and is always ready to give us a second chance. Yet that doesn't mean the way we live doesn't matter; that faith can be completely divorced from works, as though the latter is ultimately of no consequence. Works are never a *prerequisite* of faith but they should always be a *consequence* of it, what we believe and what we have experienced of God's love showing itself in some concrete way. That, I believe, is what Jesus meant by these unsettling words of his: not that we can ever hope to earn his love or merit his grace but that we need to take a long hard look at ourselves and ask whether the commitment we profess is as real as we like to imagine. To ask, in other words, whether we've understood what discipleship is all about, and whether we've actually made any place for him in our hearts at all.

Pray

Lord,
  what's happening?
Why don't you answer?
Can't you hear me?
You know who I am, surely:
  your faithful servant,

committed disciple,
loyal follower.
All right,
perhaps not that faithful, after all,
nor so committed and loyal as I might be,
but a servant nonetheless,
still a disciple and follower of Jesus,
for didn't I publicly declare my allegiance,
gladly commit myself to his cause?
Come on, Lord,
you can't deny it,
and I don't believe you'd ever want to,
so what's going on?
Why the stony silence,
this feeling I'm beating my head against a brick wall?
What's that you say? –
you don't recognise me,
don't know who I am!
But you must do!
Come on, think:
it was me in church last Sunday,
singing that hymn,
sharing that prayer,
offering those gifts.
It was me this morning,
committing the day to you,
asking for guidance,
seeking your blessing.
You *can't* have forgotten.
What do you mean, *I* forgot *you* –
failing to hear your call in the cry of my neighbour:
the groans of the hungry,
the plight of the weak,
the despair of the sick,
the pain of the lonely?
Why didn't you tell me it was you?

That's all it needed.
I'd have helped then, of course I would.
But I was in a rush to get home,
   short of loose change,
   snowed under with work,
   late for church –
   you know the sort of thing.
I never meant to shut you out,
   still less let you down.
Come on, Lord,
   be reasonable;
   you must understand.
You do, don't you?
Lord . . . ?

19
Making a difference

You are the salt of the earth . . . the light of the world . . . Let the light within you, then, shine before others, so that they may see the good deeds you do and give glory to your heavenly Father. Matthew 5:13-16

'Salt of the earth', 'light of the world' – what lovely images those are, but would anyone ever apply them to us? We'd love to think so, but the answer is probably no, there being all too little about our way of life or our discipleship that truly makes a difference to others, enriching and brightening their lives. So how can we live up to what Jesus seems to expect of us? Not through our own efforts, that's for sure. To imagine that is completely to misunderstand what he's getting at, for the light and salt he has in mind come not from us but from him. If we would show them to others, then we must first receive them ourselves, opening our lives to Christ each day so that they can flow into us and from us.

Pray

I wanted to shine, Lord,
  to live in such a way
  that people would see something different:
  a quality of love
  and generosity of spirit
  that would move them to give glory to you.
But I didn't.
The most I managed was a mere spark,
  the briefest flicker,
  kindled for a moment but then extinguished.
I wanted to be salt of the earth:
  to speak for you,

live for you,
love for you –
testifying, through my care, concern and compassion,
to your gracious purpose for all.
But, again, I didn't.
My thoughts were too much for self
and too little for you,
so that I scarcely made a difference to anyone
or anything.
I yearn to bring you glory, Lord,
but I can't do that through my own efforts
or in my own strength,
for there's nothing about me that's special,
no qualities I possess to set me apart.
It needs *you* to shine through me,
touching my heart and stirring my spirit in such a way
that I yearn to reach out in your name.
It needs you to work within me,
nurturing faith and inspiring commitment,
so that my life might bear fruit for you.
It needs you to teach me,
challenging me afresh each day with your word of life,
and helping me to listen and understand,
so that I might testify to your saving grace.
In other words,
instead of trying to shed light
I need rather to draw closer to you,
so that I may reflect *yours;*
a light that shines in the darkness,
and that nothing shall ever overcome.
Lord, hear my prayer,
and may the radiance of your presence fill me now,
in the name of Christ.
Amen.

20
Words and deeds

Take your evil deeds out of my sight! Stop doing wrong, learn to do right! Seek justice, encourage the oppressed, defend the cause of the fatherless, plead the case of the widow. Isaiah 1:16b-17

If faith cannot be reduced to works, it must nonetheless show itself in action, and nowhere should that be more so than in a commitment to justice. Poverty, hunger, disease and exploitation scar our world today as much as ever, the gap between rich and poor nations growing wider rather than smaller. Even in our own country, despite the safety net of the welfare state, life for some is a daily struggle, the opportunities most of us take for granted being a distant dream to them. We talk blithely as Christians of a time when things will be different – a time when justice will prevail, when the poor will no longer be taken advantage of, and when deprivation will be a thing of the past – but we cannot leave it there. We have a responsibility in this life to respond not just in prayer but also in deeds, doing whatever we can, no matter how small, to work for a fairer world in which the dignity and rights of all will be respected.

Pray

I speak so glibly, Lord –
  of justice for the poor,
  hope for the oppressed,
  fair shares for the exploited –
  but I rarely pause to ponder my part in their plight,
  my share of culpability for the ills of this world.

I speak of compassion for the sick,
care for the lonely,
support for the weak
and love for the outcast,
but my thoughts are focused firmly on self
and my own small world.
I find it so easy to pray,
so much harder to act;
easy to question the lifestyles of others,
so much harder to question my own;
yet whenever I act
without considering the consequences
or fail to respond from my plenty to those in need,
I deny my words through deeds,
my faith through actions,
your love through *my* complacency.
Help me to examine my discipleship honestly,
so that I may not simply talk of your concern for all,
but also show it
in all that I am
and all that I do,
to the glory of your name.
Amen.

21
Glad to give

It is more blessed to give than to receive. Acts 20:21

Is it really more blessed to give than to receive? It can be, certainly. Which of us, for example, hasn't experienced the joy of bestowing gifts on a loved one or watching children eagerly opening presents? And which hasn't felt a warm glow when giving to a good cause, being genuinely glad to show our support? Yet for most of us, myself included, giving is strictly limited, its boundaries drawn up well within what we can afford, typically restricted to our small change. To give sacrificially, so that we go without, rarely enters the equation. That, though, is what we see in Christ. He came expressly to give, laying down his life so that we might share it, sacrificing everything that we might enjoy life in all its fullness. He doesn't demand, or even expect, that we give anything in return, but he invites us freely to respond, to share in the privilege of giving not as a duty but as a joy.

Pray

I'm good at giving, Lord . . .
  in theory.
I thought, only the other day, how wonderful it would be
  to make a difference:
  to bring hope to the poor,
  food to the hungry,
  medicine to the sick
  and shelter to the homeless,
  and I resolved,
  as soon as the bank balance could stand it,
  to do something to make it happen –
  to give, and give generously.

I thought of other things besides money –
of giving my time to write to someone, ring them, visit;
my skills to help others, serve the Church,
contribute towards the community;
my energy to share someone's load, support a cause,
advance the growth of your kingdom –
only each remained just a thought,
a good intention,
time somehow always too short,
skills already called on,
energies turned inwards rather than outwards.
Forgive me, Lord,
for I've not just deprived others but myself too,
each one of us the loser.
I intended much, but achieved little,
saw the need but failed to respond,
so wrapped up in self that my so-called possessions
now in fact possess *me.*
Teach me to recognise the joy of giving,
the privilege of sharing,
the fulfilment that comes through letting go,
and so help me, in my own small way,
to offer something to others,
in grateful response to you
who gave so much for me.
Amen.

22
Hallowed be your name

. . . hallowed be your name. Matthew 6:9b

'Hallowed be your name.' We say the words, but what do we mean by them? All too easily, we repeat the phrase parrot-fashion without pausing to consider what we are saying. Perhaps the best way to understand it is to consider the trouble a multinational company takes to safeguard the standing of its brand name. No effort is spared to ensure that this is held in esteem, trusted, associated with all that is best in terms of quality, reliability and service. Similarly, hallowing means to bring glory and honour, admiration and regard. In terms of the Lord's Prayer, what we are asking for, then, is that God's name might be acknowledged, valued, held high, and if that is to happen it begins with us. If we who profess his name don't honour him, why should anyone else? If our lives don't testify to his transforming power, why should anyone take notice of the claims of the gospel? If what we practise doesn't accord with what we preach, why should anyone take our message seriously? To pray 'hallowed be your name' means to commit ourselves to doing all in our power to honour God, striving as far as is humanly possible to make our words and deeds one.

Pray

I've said it so many times, Lord –
    'hallowed be your name' –
    without ever thinking what it means.
I repeat it routinely,
    almost out of habit,

imagining that the fulfilment of those words
is down to you
rather than me.
I'm right, in part, of course,
for bringing you honour
doesn't just rest on my shoulders –
pity help you if it did!
But if I don't mean business when I pray those words,
then I've no right to pray them,
for I stand condemned by my own mouth,
exposed by my false piety.
Do I honour you? – that's the question.
Does anything in my life proclaim your kingdom,
reflect your love,
redound to your glory?
I hope so, Lord,
and I pray so,
but I know that whatever does,
far more doesn't.
So today my prayer is short and simple:
help me not just to pray that your name be honoured,
but, above all, to honour my prayer.
Amen.

23
Working for the kingdom

Your kingdom come and your will be done, on earth as it is in heaven. Matthew 6:9-10

'Your kingdom come' – we've no problem with that, for it takes us to the heart of the gospel – but can it seriously ever come 'on earth as it is in heaven'? One look at the ills that beset our world would seem to suggest otherwise. For each evil ended another begins, and for every new dawn there seems a corresponding twilight. It would be an idealist indeed who expects to see God's kingdom established in his or her lifetime, but that should not stop us from trying to bring it closer. Every deed of love we offer, every act of service, extension of forgiveness, gesture of compassion or expression of faith contributes to the fulfilment of God's purpose. These may not seem much and their impact may appear small, but they are a beginning. It's not enough simply to pray 'Your kingdom come' – God wants to know what *we* personally are doing to help bring it nearer.

Pray

Lord,
  I pray often that your will may be done
  and your kingdom come,
  but I rarely stop to consider what that involves.
It's something I ask of *you*,
  expecting *you* to accomplish it,
  you to do the spadework,
  forgetting that you need people like *me*
  to be your hands and feet,
  your agents within the world,

proclaiming the gospel,
sharing your love,
offering our service.
Forgive me, Lord,
for abdicating my share of the responsibility.
Forgive me for seeing the kingdom solely
as some future paradise,
and so ignoring the hell some endure today.
Teach me to reach out in the name of Christ,
and through my life and witness
to contribute something meaningful to your purpose,
so that a glimpse of heaven
may shine through on earth,
to your praise and glory.
Amen.

24
Transparent discipleship

Speaking the truth in love, we must grow in every respect into him, who is the head; that is, into Christ. Ephesians 4:15

Which of us can be relied on to give a straight answer to every question, even if doing so might prejudice our prospects in some way or prove uncomfortable? Which of us will own up to a mistake, admit an indiscretion or confess a fault instead of struggling desperately to cover up our tracks? It can be costly sometimes to tell the truth, and it requires wisdom and sensitivity to know when and how to speak the truth in love. The person who can be trusted to do that is a special person indeed; someone to be prized like gold dust. Is that you? It could be . . . and it *should* be.

Pray

I didn't mean to lie, Lord.
It just happened,
   the words slipping out before I had time to think.
I was embarrassed, I suppose –
   ashamed of my foolishness and failure –
   so I simply shook my head and denied the charge.
Call it instinct, if you like,
   an automatic desire to save face,
   for no one likes to be caught out,
   shown up in public,
   and that includes me as much as anyone.
But that's just the point, isn't it, Lord?
I *should* be different;
   not in any elitist sense –

smug,
sanctimonious,
self-satisfied –
but distinguished by an unpretentious honesty,
a truthfulness patent to all.
I manage that occasionally,
but less often than I'd like to think,
more typically taking refuge instead
in half-truths or white lies,
avoiding what I'd rather not face.
Yet all too easily one falsehood leads to another,
each bigger than the first,
until I find myself trapped,
caught in a snare of my own making.
Forgive me, Lord,
and grant me an upright heart and integrity of spirit.
Draw me closer to you,
and fill me with the truth that will set me free,
equipping me to live and work to your glory,
and for your kingdom.
Amen.

25
Giving our all

You shall love the Lord your God, with all your heart, all your soul, all your mind and all your strength. Deuteronomy 6:5

What does it mean to love someone? For me, three things stand out. First, it means to respond freely and spontaneously, our heart having been captured by something special we see in another. Second, it means to put that person before self, seeking their good and happiness before our own. And, third, it means to live, as far as possible, in a way that will bring pleasure, avoiding anything that might cause hurt. Is that how we relate to God? Is our relationship with him as much an affair of the heart as the mind? Do we put him first or make room for him as an afterthought? And do our lives bring him pleasure or pain, delight or dismay? We claim to love God, but is it true?

Pray

'You shall love God with heart, soul, mind and strength.'
I thought I was doing that, Lord –
  I actually believed I was offering total commitment.
When I knelt in prayer,
  sang your praises
  and studied your word,
  it was an act of worship,
  an expression of adoration.
When I brought my gifts,
  offered my service
  and shared my faith,
  it was in grateful response,
  a declaration of devotion.

I called it love,
and believed it to be just that –
my life consecrated to you –
and it *was* love, as far as it went,
but with all I feel, think and am? –
I don't think so.
What I offered involved just a small part of life,
a prescribed area set aside for you –
spiritual,
sacrosanct –
with the rest lived my way,
by my rules,
for my ends.
Forgive me, Lord,
I don't mean to shut you out,
simply seldom think to let you in,
but that's the problem:
offering a *little* of self is so easy,
offering all, so hard.
Yet that's what *you* did –
you gave everything in Christ,
your only Son,
offered freely,
gladly,
without restraint,
your love poured out for many.
I don't get near that,
but I want to try, Lord,
so, by your grace, touch my heart,
and teach me to love you
as you love me.
Amen.

26
Peacemakers

Blessed are the peacemakers, for God will call them his children.
Matthew 5:9

Nobody likes getting involved in an argument, so when controversy is in the air we tend to keep our heads down and wait for it to blow over. Better to keep the peace, we say, than stir things up. We may sometimes be right, but on occasions issues have to be addressed if there is to be any prospect of real and enduring peace rather than simply an uneasy truce. It's not easy, of course: peace-making has nothing to do with offering pat answers or cosmetic solutions, papering over the cracks to secure peace at any price. Rather, it entails a willingness to get alongside people and become involved in society in such a way that, just possibly, we can contribute to breaking down barriers, overcoming prejudice and dispelling mis-trust, creating in their place bridges of acceptance, open-ness and solidarity that enable people to work together instead of pull apart. Are we ready not just to look for peace, nor simply to long for it, but, above all, starting here and now in our daily relationships, to work to make it possible?

Pray

I wanted peace, Lord,
 an end to confrontation,
 so I bit my tongue,
 skirted the issue
 and hid my feelings.
Better that, I thought, than prolong the argument,
 allow a minor dispute to become a major row.

Yet life's not that simple –
I realise that now –
for the issue is still there,
still rankling,
still threatening to rear up and tear us apart.
It's not peace I've achieved,
but a ceasefire,
a temporary truce,
and unless we get things sorted,
thrash things out once and for all,
it's only a matter of time
before swords are drawn once more
and hostilities renewed.
Lord,
save me from declaring peace where there is no peace,
from confusing running away
with tackling the problem.
Give me the courage I need to face things head on,
sensitivity to stand in another person's shoes
and humility to listen, though I may not agree.
But teach me also,
openly and honestly,
to express my own point of view
and to engage in genuine dialogue,
speaking the truth in love.
Grant that in all my dealings,
wherever relationships are broken and emotions raw,
I might have sufficient love and concern,
patience and compassion,
to be a peacemaker –
an agent of your reconciliation,
in the name of Christ.
Amen.

27
Dealing with anger

Get rid of all bitterness, rage, temper, backbiting and insults, together with all malicious thoughts, and instead show kindness to one another, compassion and mercy, forgiving each other just as God has forgiven you in Christ. Ephesians 4:31-32

Even the most placid of us feel angry sometimes – it's part of being human; even Jesus was roused to an explosion of fury in the Jerusalem temple. Confronted by evil, injustice and exploitation, anger is not only understandable but necessary. More commonly, however, especially if we allow it to fester within us, its effect is destructive, leading to consequences that both we and others regret. Unless we are able to control anger before it controls us, then we are like a child unwittingly toying with an unexploded bomb. Next time, then, you feel the red mist rising, stop, count to ten, consider the consequences and give yourself time to cool down.

Pray

Was I wrong to be angry, Lord?
I really don't know.
I thought at the time I was justified,
  my rage understandable,
  and, if anything, I was more restrained
  than I might have been.
But now –
  with time to reflect,
  ponder,
  see things from the other side –
  I'm not so sure,
  wondering, perhaps, if fury blinded me to reason;

my response as much due to selfishness,
wounded pride,
bigotry,
as any sense of justice.
Whatever the case,
warranted or not,
I was wrong in what followed:
spitting out cruel, callous words,
designed to wound,
vent my spleen,
rather than resolve the argument.
And then, to fan the flames,
raking over the coals day by day –
that was unforgivable,
for it was no longer fed by white-hot emotion,
but cold and calculated,
petty vindictiveness rather than righteous indignation.
Forgive me, Lord,
and help me to heal the wounds I've caused
and the hurt I've given.
Teach me that anger has its place,
but only as a tool for good,
never a weapon for evil;
and grant me wisdom to know the difference
and to show it in all my dealings,
for Christ's sake.
Amen.

GROWTH IN GRACE

28
Prepared to grow

Speaking the truth in love, we will in every respect grow into the one who is the Head; that is, Christ, in whom the whole body is assembled and held together by the ligaments he supplies for it, and through whom each part is able to function as it should so that the body can grow as it builds itself up in love.
Ephesians 4:15-16

Age, we are told, brings wisdom. Well, perhaps, but it's by no means guaranteed, for it all depends on the experiences a person has and a willingness to learn from them. Some features characteristic of advancing years may come automatically, but maturity is not among them. Similarly, maturity in Christ is not something we should take for granted, assuming it arises routinely as a direct consequence of the years we've been a Christian. If we are to grow in faith, we need first the desire to do so and second the resolve to help it happen. It depends ultimately on Christ, for without his nurture, encouragement and inspiration, faith is doomed to wither and die. In turn, though, he needs our cooperation: a willingness to make time for quiet reflection and devotion, a readiness to listen and learn, a genuine hunger and thirst for righteousness. Christian discipleship is not just about a one-off act of commitment but about an ongoing relationship, an unfolding story, a continuing process of growth.

Pray

I still used the right language, Lord,
still talked of growing in grace,
bearing fruit,
attaining maturity in Christ,

but the facts spoke otherwise –
my discipleship not just standing still
but in danger of terminal decline.
It wasn't meant to happen, of course,
but I'd grown careless,
complacent,
forgetting that faith needs to be nourished
and nurtured
if it is not to shrivel up and die.
Thankfully, you called me back,
renewing as you have done so many times before;
my appetite restored
such that I yearned to know you better,
to explore the breadth, length, height and depth
of your love in Christ –
but I'd been close to losing faith,
to falling away –
too close.
Forgive me, Lord, for being content
simply to drift along.
Forgive my casualness in discipleship
and complacency in worship;
my leaving everything to you as if I've no part to play.
Teach me that,
however much I have understood of your greatness
or experienced of your love,
I have barely begun to explore the whole,
and so help me grow,
not just today but every day,
to the glory of your name.
Amen.

29
Fruitful faith

The fruits of the Spirit are love, joy, peace, tolerance, generosity, reliability, gentleness and self-control. Galatians 5:22

What sorts of fruits characterise our lives? Do people look at us and see the kinds of qualities Paul wrote of in his letter to the Galatians, or are other fruits more in evidence: bitterness, jealousy, anger, pride, tetchiness, intolerance? The reality, for most of us, is that we produce a mixture of good and bad fruit, being faithful in some things and faithless in others, but the latter prevails over the former more often than we would like. What can we do about it? We can try to change, of course, and may to a point succeed, but anyone who has tried making New Year resolutions will know that it's more easily said than done. Real change is finally dependent on God's grace, working within us through Christ to make us new. It is only through growing closer to him – the true vine – that we can become the people that both we and he want us to be.

Pray

It's not much of a harvest, Lord, is it?
Not when you think of the years you've nurtured me,
the way you've so patiently and lovingly
tended my faith,
seeking to cultivate fruits of your Spirit
able to nourish others in turn.
Not that I've been barren –
at least *that's* true –
occasional deeds of love,
acts of kindness

and gestures of compassion
offering testimony to your creative touch,
your life-giving hand at work.
But those have been all too few,
a mere taste of the rich harvest you yearn to see.
It's not for want of trying, Lord,
you know that.
If anything, I've tried too hard,
believing that through sheer willpower
I can yield a harvest,
good intentions enough to produce good fruit.
Forgive me, Lord,
for I got it wrong,
imagining *I* could achieve what is down to *you.*
Forgive me for seeing myself as the vine
rather than simply a branch,
dependent on you for sustenance,
strength and support.
Come now, and promote growth
from the fresh shoots of faith.
Prune away whatever is sterile,
and feed what is sound,
so that my life may blossom anew
and be truly fruitful,
to the glory of your name.
Amen.

GRACE
AND MERCY

30
Trust in God's transforming power

Anyone united with Christ is a new creation; the old self has passed away in its entirety; everything is made new. 2 Corinthians 5:17

It's one thing to recognise that all is not as it should be, quite another to put things right. In discipleship that's as true as anywhere. Most of us are ready to acknowledge our faults, but when it comes to changing for the better we wring our hands in despair. We've all tried and failed too often. Yet that, of course, is to forget Paul's words to the Corinthians, his reminder that, in Christ, we are a new creation, the old done away with, put behind us. Though our daily experience of failure may seem to contradict this, God is nonetheless constantly at work within us, transforming, redeeming and renewing. If we could only open our lives more fully to him, seeking his will and responding to his guidance, we would experience yet more fully his transforming power. What *we* cannot change, *he* can.

Pray

I can't change, Lord!
I'd like to,
  and I try to,
  but you can see for yourself,
  after all these years,
  that it's no good,
  my every attempt doomed to failure,
  my intentions good but the results feeble.
I've done my best, heaven knows,
  striving every day to follow you more faithfully,

but all my efforts have come to nothing,
the spirit willing but the flesh weak.
Yet, what am I saying?
I'm wrong again,
for it's not down to me –
my resolve,
my will –
but to your grace,
your redeeming, renewing touch;
you alone able to change the inside,
to effect a new creation,
to take what is and shape what will be.
Forgive me, Lord, for yet again turning faith into works,
confusing what is impossible for me
with what is possible with you.
Forgive me for losing sight
of your transforming power and restoring love.
Draw me closer to you,
so that you may work within me,
taking what I am and, by your grace,
fashioning what I may yet become,
to the glory of your name.
Amen.

31
Trust in God's patience

You are forgiving, O Lord, a merciful God, dependable, slow to anger, and overflowing in patience. Psalm 86:15

No matter how patient we are, there comes a point when we've had enough; when, unable to restrain ourselves any longer, we explode in anger or frustration. We don't mind putting up with the occasional irritation, the odd mistake, but when someone goes on committing the same error *ad infinitum* something inside finally snaps. Understandably, we tend to assume that God reacts in the same way. For all our talk of his limitless grace and unbounded love, we find it hard to imagine he thinks any differently, and, in consequence, the more we fail the more burdened we become by a sense of guilt. If that's you, stop and think again, for ours is a God who forgives and goes on forgiving, his patience never exhausted and his grace never spent. You may make the same mistakes today you've always made, exhibit the same flaws, fall prey to the same temptations – God is still ready to pardon. Yes, our failure will grieve him, and, yes, he will hope for better things, but as long as we are truly sorry, then his nature is always to show mercy.

Pray

'Oh no! Not again!'
I don't know about you, Lord,
 but that's what I felt like saying:
 uttering a howl of despair,
 groan of frustration,
 as once more I made the same mistake,
 displaying the same weakness,

the same flaw,
as so many times before.
Could you still have patience,
still forgive?
I know I couldn't.
I'd have long since lashed out in fury
or simply walked away,
such persistent folly and feeble resolve
too much to bear.
Yet not you, Lord.
Somehow,
despite it all,
you reach out, time and again, with the same welcome,
the same warmth,
ready once more to let bygones be bygones,
to put the past behind me and let me start afresh.
I don't understand such forbearance,
such grace,
such love,
but I praise you for it,
for in you alone I find one ready to see the worst
and yet believe the best,
to see what I am
and still keep faith in what I might become.
Lord, for bearing with me,
for your awesome, amazing patience,
receive my heartfelt undying thanks,
in the name of Christ.
Amen.

32
Prepared to receive

In this is love, not that we loved God but that he loved us and sent his Son to be the expiation for our sins. 1 John 4:10

If it is more blessed to give than to receive, it can correspondingly be harder to receive than to give, which perhaps explains why we struggle sometimes to accept the simple message at the heart of the gospel: God's gift of forgiveness and new life through his Son. 'OK,' we say, 'where's the catch?' We simply cannot help assuming that we must do something to earn God's forgiveness, the idea of getting something for nothing alien to our understanding of the world. Yet God's love has no hidden clauses; it's there for the taking, extended to all, needing only our willingness to reach out and receive it. He loved us before we ever loved him, and when we open our hearts to Christ, however flawed our response may be, we open a conduit for him to pour that love into our hearts. The gift is for all, no strings attached. Have you received it?

Pray

Amazing grace –
  that's what I speak of, Lord,
  that's what I claim for you:
  a gift offered freely,
  no strings attached,
  no price to pay.
It sounds wonderful,
  except that I don't really believe it,
  my life making that all too clear,
  whatever my words may say.

You love me, I imagine,
as long as I go to church,
say my prayers,
read your word.
You accept me as long as I believe the accepted dogma,
recite the established creed,
conform to the particular statement of faith.
You forgive me as long as I'm essentially honest,
decent,
respectable –
the sort of person you'd care to mix with.
You bless me, in other words, as long as I bless you,
scratching my back provided I scratch yours first,
your goodness conditional
on my doing, believing and being the right thing.
I don't say it, of course,
but I think it,
or others tell me it's what I should think,
and so gift becomes graft,
joy becomes duty,
what should be mine to *receive*
becoming instead mine to *earn*.
Lord,
forgive me for imposing my ways on you,
my values and expectations.
Forgive me for limiting your love
to the pale imitation I struggle to offer.
Above all, though, thank you
for continuing to reach out to me each day,
accepting me despite my getting it wrong,
devoted to me despite my lack of devotion to you,
loving me with your awesome, amazing grace!
Amen.

33
Purity of heart

Blessed are those whose hearts are pure; they will see God.
Matthew 5:8

What do we mean when we speak of being pure in heart? Typically this seems to be equated to moral uprightness, but I don't think this idea begins to cover everything Jesus had in mind. In daily parlance, the word 'pure' means that something is pristine – nothing added or taken away; 100 per cent what it claims to be. It's not hard to see how that might relate to Christian discipleship. Understood thus, the call to be pure asks searching questions concerning our thoughts and attitudes, our innermost motives for acting, thinking and speaking as we do. Is who and what we are in tune with God, totally at one with his will? Or are our words and deeds tarnished by greed, envy, lust, bitterness, pride? Are we 100 per cent committed to God, so that we strive in every aspect of our lives to honour him? The more we attain such purity of heart; such undivided, undiluted commitment, the more we will indeed see God, for *we* will be one with him and *he* one with us.

Pray

I thought I was getting close, Lord;
  that at least, if not controlling them entirely,
  I was on top of my impure thoughts,
  able to nip them in the bud
  before they fully took hold.
It may not sound much
  but for me it was an achievement,
  for it doesn't come easily;

lust, greed, deceit and envy all too much a part of me –
hard to resist,
easy to excuse.
I've avoided those, Lord –
most of the time, anyway –
my thoughts turned, as far as I could make them,
on what is good,
pleasing,
true,
honouring to you.
Yet while that, if only in part, was purity of *mind,*
it was not purity of *heart,*
for it was a daily struggle,
an uphill battle to conquer my inclinations
and control my impulses,
to be what I wish I was
rather than what I am.
It's a start, isn't it? –
but I'll never achieve that goal in my own strength,
only through your grace.
So draw me closer, Lord,
and, in your love, work within me.
Wash me,
and I shall be whiter than snow.
Touch me,
and I shall be clean.
Put a new heart and a right spirit within me,
so that I may delight to do your will
and yearn to honour you always.
Take what I am,
and direct what I shall be,
to your glory.
Amen.

34
Avoiding temptation

Keep alert, and pray that you will not fall into temptation; the spirit may be willing but the flesh is weak. Matthew 26:41

Does temptation strike out of the blue? Well, it may do sometimes, but more often than not it finds weak spots that we are well aware of, pressure points where we know we are vulnerable. We all have an Achilles' heel somewhere – that place where temptation is strongest. Do we carry on regardless, deliberately courting trouble? Do we knowingly put ourselves in situations where we are likely to fall? If so, we need to take steps to avoid them before it's too late, to do all we can to avoid putting obstacles in our path. The way of Christ is narrow and difficult; if we make it narrower still, then we've only ourselves to blame.

Pray

I fell, Lord,
  let you down completely,
  and I'm sorry for that,
  ashamed of my weakness,
  the frailty of my commitment.
But I'm more sorry still that I set myself up to fall,
  knowingly putting myself in a situation
  where my weaknesses were exposed
  and temptation was bound to strike,
  almost impossible to resist.
I knew the dangers,
  and should have steered clear,
  but I was torn in two,

part of me yearning to do your will
but the greater part half-wishing to succumb
to the tempter's voice,
to indulge in forbidden fruit.
I suppose I thought it wouldn't matter;
that you'd overlook the occasional lapse,
forgive the odd transgression,
just as you've done so many times before.
And so you will,
no question,
your nature always to have mercy,
to pick me up and help me start again –
provided, that is, I still look for forgiveness,
still want to walk in your way.
But that's the crunch,
for if I give in today,
the chances are I'll give in tomorrow and the next day,
slowly losing sight of your will,
forgetting what it means to follow you,
drifting ever-further from your side.
Forgive me, Lord,
and call me back before it's too late.
Give me strength not just to resist temptation
but also to avoid whatever might cause me to fall,
and so may I stay true to you
as you are invariably true to me,
through Jesus Christ my Lord.
Amen.

35
Prepared to say sorry

If we claim to have no sin, we are fooling ourselves and the truth has no place in us. If we confess our sins, God is just, and we can rely on him to forgive our sins and cleanse us from all evil. 1 John 1:8-9

'Anyone who makes a mistake and fails to acknowledge it, commits another' – so run the wise words of the Chinese philosopher Confucius. If that's true in relation to others, it's all the more so when it comes to God. If we are to find forgiveness and be able to start again, we need to recognise and own up to what is wrong in our lives. This means more, though, than simply offering vague confession – anyone can do that, but it doesn't get us very far. True confession means taking a long hard look at ourselves and acknowledging where we might be found wanting. It means listening to God's challenge, from wherever it might come and being open to having our comfortable preconceptions and assumptions challenged. Such a searching examination can be hugely painful, but it is also the pathway to inner healing and wholeness, to a peace beyond human understanding, to new life in Christ.

Pray

I prayed, Lord,
    asking forgiveness for all that was wrong in my life,
    all the ways I'd failed you,
    and I thought that was an end to it:
    that I'd made my confession
    and received your pardon.

To a point I was right,
for you *had* forgiven –
gladly,
freely,
wholeheartedly –
yet there were so many faults that I hadn't confessed,
hadn't even begun to acknowledge,
and much though you longed
to release me from those too,
you couldn't touch them –
couldn't bring me the healing, wholeness,
renewal and restoration you so yearned for me to enjoy.
They will imprison me still –
denying,
destroying –
until I recognise their presence,
and bring them before you,
for only then can you draw their poison,
cleanse the wounds
and heal the scars.
Forgive me, Lord, for having taken the easy way –
acknowledging general wrongdoing
rather than specific errors,
offering sweeping confession
rather than genuine remorse.
Forgive me for confusing
a vague acceptance of guilt
with a searching and sincere identification
of my weaknesses.
Give me honesty and humility to recognise my faults,
and to confess them with genuine sorrow,
so that I may receive your healing, renewing touch.
Amen.

36
Prepared to *be* sorry

Confess your sins to one another. James 5:16

It's often noted that sorry is the hardest word to say, few of us relishing the prospect of acknowledging our mistakes, but if *saying* sorry is difficult, *being* sorry is harder still. Words alone are meaningless unless they are reinforced by actions. We have to want to change, doing our best to avoid making the same mistake again. We may not always succeed, but it should at least be evident that we are trying to put right those things in our lives that we know to be wrong. Is that true of you? When you apologise for something – an unkind word, a foolish action, a careless mistake – do you strive to ensure that it never happens again? When you offer confession to God, do you do so resolved to try harder to conquer temptation when it comes next time, to overcome that weakness of yours that caused you to fall, to follow Christ more faithfully in the days ahead? In other words, whenever you say sorry, are you prepared also to *be* sorry?

Pray

I still haven't learned, Lord, have I?
I've made progress –
    a little anyway –
    recognising and confessing my faults,
    but that's about as far as it goes.
Though I've *said* sorry,
    I've not actually *shown* it –
    neither to you nor to others –
    and, to my shame, I've scarcely even tried.

I thought words were all it took,
one simple expression of regret
sufficient to put things right,
but I realise now that pious sentiments are not enough,
exposed as hollow,
empty,
meaningless,
unless there's something more solid to back them up,
some attempt to mend my ways,
live differently,
correct what I know to be wrong.
I may not succeed in that –
not even get anywhere close –
but unless I at least attempt to change
I can say sorry as often as I like
and few will take notice,
for though my lips will say one thing
my life will profess another.
Teach me, then, not just to confess my faults
but also to strive, as far as it lies within me,
to overcome them;
to express remorse not just in words but in deeds.
Teach me to *be* sorry,
in the name of Christ.
Amen.

37
Forgive and forget

. . . forgive our mistakes as we forgive those who wrong us.
Matthew 6:12

What do we make of those words of Jesus? Is God's forgiveness conditional on our forgiving others? It can't be, for if it were we'd all be in a sorry pass. Moreover, it would make God's love dependent on works rather than faith. Yet, if nothing else, we must surely aim to forgive, even if we fail. True remorse shows itself in a desire to change, to show that our expression of regret is more than simply empty words; and, according to Jesus, the best way to do that – perhaps, even, the only way – is to forgive others in turn. If the intention to do that isn't there, then we risk denying ourselves God's forgiveness, not because he withholds it but because we haven't grasped what it means and so are unable to make it ours. Next time, then, you come before God, seeking his mercy, begging for pardon, stop and ask yourself whether others are asking the same of you, and whether you've really understood what forgiveness is all about.

Pray

I meant to forgive, Lord,
  to put the past behind me and start afresh . . .
  and I honestly thought I had.
But I see now that I was wrong,
  for I've raked things up again;
  mistakes long past,
  which I thought were dead and buried,
  plucked from the ashes,
  rekindled,
  and hurled in bitter accusation.

It was a shock, Lord,
for I truly believed I'd dealt with the matter,
any last flickering flame of anger finally extinguished,
but somewhere, deep within,
the embers were still smouldering,
needing only a little more fuel to reignite them.
It's more complicated than I imagined,
this business of offering real, unreserved pardon,
for hurt and bitterness are hard to quench,
but I need to douse the blaze once and for all,
for it's consuming my relationships,
not just with others
but, worst of all, with you.
Have mercy, Lord, and by your grace
replace the cinders of anger and resentment
with the fire of love.
May your grace and mercy burn within me,
so that I might learn to forgive
as you have so faithfully forgiven,
showing the same gracious and generous pardon
that you so freely offer to all,
through Jesus Christ my Lord.
Amen.

THE JOURNEY OF DISCIPLESHIP

38
A continuing response

We need, then, to pay ever more attention to everything we have heard, to ensure that we do not wander from it. Hebrews 2:1

A while back I took up visiting a local gym, determined to get myself into better shape. For the first month or so I went along three or four times a week . . . then once or twice a week . . . but more recently it has been closer to once a month. Apparently this is by no means atypical. All across the country, so I'm told, innumerable people enlist in a surge of athletic enthusiasm, only for most to give up within six months. If nothing else, then, I can claim to have stayed the course longer than most! When it comes to discipleship, initial enthusiasm can similarly start to wane. What started off so vibrantly can become a matter of habit, duty, going through the motions. Indeed, that's almost inevitable unless we take the time to nurture our relationship with God, so that faith can be continually nourished and strengthened. True discipleship is not about occasional bursts of fervour but about a lifetime of dedication, running the race with perseverance. Short-term commitment is one thing, long-term devotion quite another. Which of those two might best be used to describe our response to the good news of Jesus Christ?

Pray

Lord,
  it all seemed so easy at the time –
  a personal response,
  a public act of commitment,
  and it was done,

my colours nailed to the mast,
a Christian for all to see.
Only, of course, that wasn't the end to it but the beginning,
the start of a twisting and sometimes testing road,
calling for resilience,
dedication,
perseverance.
I've walked it, Lord,
and want to keep on walking,
but you know that at times I've faltered,
stumbled,
lost my way,
even, on occasions, taken several steps back,
and I worry that one day I might fall altogether –
the way too hard,
the challenge too steep,
the lure of other paths too strong to resist.
Save me from that, I pray.
Walk with me, even if I go astray,
pick me up should I fall,
strengthen me should my spirit fail,
and so may I press on until I reach my journey's end,
the goal to which you have called me heavenward
through Jesus Christ my Lord.
Amen.

39
Pathway to life

Proceed through the narrow gate. Many choose the wide gate instead, but that path leads only to ruin. By contrast, the path that leads to life is straight and narrow, and is found by just a handful. Matthew 7:13-14

Confronted by choices in life, nine times out of ten we will opt for the path that asks the least of us, the way that ensures that the *status quo* is disturbed as little as possible. Of course, that easy option need not necessarily be the wrong one, any more than the hard option must always prove right, but surprisingly often committed discipleship involves difficult decisions and costly challenges: turning the other cheek, loving our enemies, going the extra mile, being willing, if necessary, even to be persecuted for the cause of Christ. That's the sort of challenge entering through the narrow gate involves. More than simply committing ourselves to Christ, it means being ready to take difficult decisions that frequently will run counter to the normative values of society. The temptation to turn back and take the less gruelling path will always be there, beguiling us with the idea that there are various paths to the same goal. It is easy to set off along the narrow way, far harder to continue to the end.

Pray

Forgive me, Lord,
    for I took the easy path once again, didn't I?
I didn't mean to,
    or so I tell myself;
    it's just that life was fraught,
    difficult,
    demanding –

so much to get done,
so many problems to sort out –
and so I decided, just the once,
to take the comfortable route,
the least taxing path,
promising that next time would be different.
Only that's what I said last time . . .
and the time before . . .
and the time before that:
forever resolving that one day,
when the moment is right,
I'll face the challenge,
walk more faithfully the way of Christ,
grapple with what it means to carry my cross.
It's not enough, I see that now,
for the reason the way is narrow is *because* it's hard;
because following you entails tough decisions,
awkward choices,
here and now,
in all the hurly-burly of life,
the pressures and responsibilities of the daily routine.
It won't be easier tomorrow or the next day,
for it's not meant to be –
discipleship involving costly loving, giving and serving –
and if I keep on ducking the issue until the time is right,
I'll go on doing so for ever,
taking the wide gate by default,
the path that leads to ruin.
Forgive me, Lord,
and, by your grace, help me to change.
Help me, starting from this moment,
when faced by the need to decide,
to choose not the easy way
but *your* way,
however challenging that might be.
Amen.

40
Don't be deceived

Watch out for bogus prophets. Outwardly, they may seem as innocent as sheep, but deep down they are slavering wolves. Their fruits will give them away. Matthew 7:15-16a

Who are the bogus prophets of today? There are obvious candidates: peddlers of drugs and pornography, promoters of religious cults and offbeat sects, self-styled gurus and seers to name but some; but the chief threat, I suspect, is far more insidious than any of these. It is not any one person or group of people, but rather society at large, or, if you prefer, peer pressure. Each day we are surrounded by assumptions, ideas, suggestions and preconceptions that all too easily shape the way we think, slowly but surely conforming us to the way of this world rather than the way of Christ. Without us even being aware of it, the pressure to go along with the crowd is constantly being applied in myriad ways, touching on almost every aspect of life. The threat here is strongest because it is the least obvious. Where temptation is clear, it is easier to resist, but when it comes in obscure guises, it is hard to recognise, let alone combat. Beware of all that surreptitiously may nibble away at your faith, eroding your convictions, undermining your principles and indiscernibly leading you away from Christ. Whoever you are, the danger is more real than you might think.

Pray

Was I taken in, Lord?
Partly, perhaps,
  a bit of me fooled by the persuasive arguments,
  the attractive, alluring promises.

But much of me,
  deep down,
  wanted to be deceived:
  to hear what I wanted to hear
  and see what I wanted to see.
I was looking for an excuse, I suppose –
  a way of making discipleship a little easier,
  a fraction less demanding,
  for though I talk casually of sacrifice,
  of walking the way of the cross,
  I find the idea daunting;
  surrendering *anything* hard enough,
  let alone my all.
I'm just too human, that's the truth of it,
  my ways not your ways
  nor my thoughts your thoughts,
  and the tension shows,
  impossible to hide.
I want to do your will,
  but want *mine* as well.
I hunger for treasure in heaven,
  but thirst equally for riches on earth.
I mean to turn from evil,
  yet can't resist temptation.
I resolve to serve others,
  but end up serving self.
Time and again, Lord, the gulf is exposed,
  and it hurts to face that challenge,
  so I shut it out,
  stopping my ears to whatever might disturb,
  listening instead to a more comfortable gospel,
  accommodated to my needs,
  promising gain without pain,
  all the rewards with none of the cost.
Forgive me, Lord,
  and save me from settling for a peace

where there is no peace,
a life which is no life,
a 'truth' that is false.
Teach me to listen to your voice,
however testing your call,
and to follow where you lead,
however hard the path,
for you alone can offer food that satisfies,
fulfilment that endures,
hope that shall not fail
and joy for all eternity.
Amen.

41
Seeing it through

So then, since we are surrounded by so great a cloud of witnesses, let us discard everything that encumbers us and the sin that clings so closely; and let us run with perseverance the race set before us. Hebrews 12:1

There are times, aren't there, when we wish we could put the clock back and start again. As the old saying has it, 'Act in haste, repent at leisure'. Some can feel precisely this in relation to Christ. Having committed themselves to him in a momentary impulse, they wonder afterwards exactly what it is they have taken on. The fact is that discipleship involves more than a one-off decision; it entails, rather, a continuing journey that calls for vigilance and dedication. That's why the writer to the Hebrews, having reminded his readers of the birth of Christ that set in motion the events of the gospel, went on to emphasise the importance of finishing what they'd started. We in turn may feel sometimes, faced by the cost of discipleship, that we have bitten off more than we can chew. We may find the implications of discipleship far more demanding than we ever anticipated and wonder just what it is that we've got ourselves into. Yet, however often we may fail, the invitation is always there to begin again, not alone but with Christ by our side. With his help we will find the strength we need to honour the commitment we have made.

Pray

It seemed a good idea at the time, Lord,
 not just the right thing to do, but the only thing.
You called
 and I responded,
 freely,

thankfully,
gladly,
the joy of your love flooding my soul,
the promise of new life stretching out gloriously before me.
I'd made my decision,
and I was happy to have done so,
confident of the way ahead.
Only then the doubts started,
not about you but me,
my ability to honour the promise I'd made.
It wasn't that my love changed – don't think that –
simply that I began to understand
what commitment involves.
Your call to love and go on loving,
to give and go on giving,
to turn the other cheek,
forgive my enemies,
walk the extra mile –
I hadn't bargained on those,
and, together, they've made me realise
that taking a decision is one thing,
living up to it quite another.
I'm scared, Lord,
afraid of letting you down,
of promising much but achieving little,
my faith all show and no substance.
I want to follow, you know that –
but I'm not sure I have the courage or dedication
I need to see it through.
Oh Lord, what have I done?
Where am I going?
You helped me decide;
now help me live with my decision!
Amen.

JUDGING OTHERS

42
Who are we to judge?

If you don't want to be judged, don't sit in judgement on others, for you will be judged by the same yardstick, evaluated according to the evaluation you yourself employ.
Matthew 7:1

The Bible has a lot to say about judging others, repeatedly warning us against doing so, yet all too often the Church has been a seedbed of bigotry, narrow-mindedness, intolerance and hypocrisy. Religion, like politics, arouses strong feelings, convictions becoming so entrenched that anyone who dares question them is condemned without a second hearing. Some, further, see it as their God-given duty to safeguard moral standards and are afraid that if the edges are once blurred, then moral chaos will follow. Yet, if we could but see it, this, once again, is making the cardinal mistake of setting ourselves up as God. Certainly, we must live as we believe he calls us to, but that shouldn't mean imposing on others the requirement to do the same. The one commandment that we should focus on above all others is that of Jesus to love one another. If only we as Christians could do just that, putting the time we spend in judging others into loving them instead, this world would be an infinitely happier place, and the cause of Christ would be advanced beyond our wildest imagining.

Pray

I can't help judging, Lord.
I need to make up my mind
  about the rights and wrongs of a situation,
  about people's actions and the motives behind them,

about whether things are acceptable or unacceptable,
good or evil.
If I didn't do that I'd be weak, foolish, naïve,
lacking in principles or conviction,
easy prey for the unscrupulous.
It goes wider than that, though,
for there are times too when, as a society,
we need to pass judgement,
literally,
sentencing those who break the law,
who hurt, destroy, wound or kill,
for how else can we safeguard the well-being of all?
So it doesn't come easily,
understanding these words of yours,
recognising how they might apply to daily life,
to this world as we know it.
Yet I can see clearly enough
that it's one thing to believe an action is wrong,
quite another to set myself up as sole judge and jury;
one thing to have reservations
about someone's words or actions,
altogether different to write them off entirely.
You do not say there's no such thing as judgement,
still less play down the distinction
between good or evil,
but what you do say is that it's not for me
to pronounce the final verdict;
that is down to you alone.
Save me, then, from narrow judgemental attitudes,
from the assumption that I am right
and others are wrong.
Save me from seeing the faults in others
but being blind to those within myself.
Give me a spirit that builds people up
rather than tearing them down;
that discerns the good

rather than dwelling on the bad;
that brings out the best
rather than highlighting the worst.
Teach me to love instead of passing judgement on others,
just as you have so wonderfully
and unreservedly
loved me.
Amen.

43
A second look

I pray this . . . that Christ may so dwell in your hearts through faith that you will be able to grasp with all the saints the breadth, length, height and depth of the love of Christ, and that you may know this all-surpassing love in such a way that you may be filled with the very fullness of God.
Ephesians 3:14a, 17-19

'A little knowledge', so they say, 'is a dangerous thing.' The problem, of course, is that when we know a little we can sometimes imagine we know it all. Paradoxically, the more we learn about a particular subject the more we realise how much we still don't understand. The same holds true in our relationships, both with others and with God. We can all too easily make judgements about people based on the flimsiest of evidence, once again assuming we know all there is to know, or worse still, imagining we know everything, or near enough everything about God. In each case, it is a dangerous mistake to make. Why? Because our knowledge is flawed – there is almost certainly more to every person than meets the eye, and quite definitely far more to God than we can ever even begin to comprehend. A wise person is always aware that their knowledge is partial, that there is more to be revealed, more to learn, more to understand.

Pray

It was a shock, Lord.
I thought I knew him inside out,
  understanding, as well as any, what made him tick,
  the sort of person he was.

But he took me by surprise,
showing a side to his character I never knew existed,
qualities I wouldn't have believed possible,
depths I hadn't even dreamt of.
The mistake was mine, of course.
To presume, even for a moment,
that I could know all there was to know,
grasp the whole truth rather than just a fraction,
was foolish of me,
quite wrong.
for what I thought was comprehension
actually blinded me to reality,
obscuring what I could and would have seen
if only I'd been open to what was there before me.
Lord,
save me from doing the same with you,
from mistakenly believing my faith is complete,
my knowledge of you total.
Prevent me from limiting what you are
to what I conceive you to be,
from restricting the way you can shape my life
to the way I expect you to work,
from confusing my partial grasp of your grace
with the full wonder of the gospel.
Keep me always open
to fresh insights and deeper understanding,
to a richer and fuller revelation of truth.
Whatever light I have glimpsed,
remind me that there is more to break through.
Open my eyes, then, each day to see and know you better,
until that time
when I enter into the radiance of your presence
and meet you face to face.
Amen.

44
Skin deep

The Lord does not see as people see, for they look at appearances, but he sees rather into the heart. 1 Samuel 16:7b

Fans of the celebrated TV series *Fawlty Towers* may well remember a hilarious episode when a youthful 'medallion man' arrives, shirt unbuttoned to the waist to reveal his macho and hairy torso. In a trice Basil Fawlty sums him up as an unsophisticated lout, little more than a monkey, in complete contrast to the genteel and cultured Lord Melbury, whose immaculate attire speaks for itself. The reality, however, turns out to be different, Melbury is exposed as a conman whom 'monkey man' – in reality a plain-clothes policeman – has been tracking for some time. It's a brilliant spoof, but sadly the superficial judgements it parodies are all too real, our conclusions about people frequently based on first impressions or outward appearances. The words of God to Samuel remind us of the need to look deeper to the person underneath.

Pray

It looked delicious, Lord –
ripe,
succulent,
appetising –
so I took a bite . . .
and spat it out in disgust.
I should have known better, of course;
should have realised long ago
that appearances aren't everything,
yet, somehow, the message never seems to get through.

It's almost as though I can't help myself,
 a pleasant exterior all it takes to win me over,
 and when what's underneath
 fails to measure up to my expectations
 I express surprise,
 dismay,
 even anger,
 scarcely able to conceal my disbelief.
Lord, it may not matter much with fruit,
 but it does when it comes to people –
 when I'm duped by outward show
 and taken in by a pretty face,
 when my attitudes are coloured
 by superficial impressions
 so that I presume to pass judgement
 on what I don't understand.
Help me, then, to see not with my eyes but yours,
 and to catch a glimpse, behind the façade,
 to the person within.
Amen.

45
Respect for all

There is now neither Jew nor Greek, slave nor free, male nor female, for you are all one in Christ. Galatians 3:28

Are we open to others? No doubt we all like to think so, but differences of outlook and belief, viewpoint and character can estrange us from other people more than we might imagine, closing our minds to meaningful dialogue or a genuine meeting of minds. It was equally so in the time of Christ, perhaps more so, Gentiles, women, lepers and tax-collectors, to name but some, all victims of prejudice and discrimination. Times may have moved on today, but bigotry and intolerance are still to be found, all too many denied their rights, even persecuted, due to inflexible and small-minded preconceptions. Contrast that with Christ, the man for others: a man who broke through the social, religious, cultural and racial barriers of his time, demonstrating that God's love extends to all. In a predominantly insular society, a still divided Church and an increasingly unstable world, we need to hear that message more than ever. Whoever we are, we need to ask whether we're as open to others as we like to think we are; as open as God would have us be.

Pray

Lord,
  I try not to be prejudiced,
  and, in terms of the major issues at least –
  issues like race, gender and the like –
  I think most of the time I succeed.
Yet there's more to it than that, isn't there?

For, in a host of other ways,
  I still sum people up on the flimsiest of evidence,
  allowing vague assumptions to shape
  not just my perception
  but even sometimes my attitude and actions.
I observe the way people dress, look, speak and act,
  and look no further.
I get wind of their politics, convictions and beliefs,
  and bracket them accordingly.
Time and again, instead of reality, I deal in stereotypes,
  unable to see past the label to the person underneath.
Yet you see us as we are,
  each with our mix of good and bad,
  strengths and weaknesses,
  yet valuing every one of us as a unique individual,
  precious in your sight.
Forgive me, Lord,
  those times I have lost sight of people's distinctiveness,
  their innate worth as human beings.
Forgive me when I have failed to give them
  the respect they deserve,
  pigeonholing rather than interacting,
  assessing according to conjecture and preconceptions
  instead of weighing up the facts.
Deliver me, Lord, from all the ways
  prejudice still poisons my relationships,
  so that I may recognise the true worth of all.
In your name I ask it.
Amen.

RESPONDING IN FAITH

46
Time to decide

If you would rather not serve the Lord, then choose this day whom you will serve. Joshua 24:15a

For all of us, in faith as in life, there comes a time to decide. For some it might be the challenge to commit their life to Christ. For others it might be the call to service or a position of leadership, while for others still it might be to a change of lifestyle, an acknowledgement of mistakes, or a resolve to begin again. Whatever it is, we can be tempted to push such questions aside, hoping they'll go away. All in good time, we tell ourselves; we can deal with such things when there are less pressing matters to concern ourselves with. And so we go on postponing a decision to another day, just as we have done so many times before. There is no peace that way, however; we will simply condemn ourselves to struggle on with the burden of that unresolved question. Worse still, we may put off a response altogether, or find, when we get round to it, that the opportunity has passed us by. Better by far to consider carefully and prayerfully what is being asked of us. Is it simply the voice of ambition, wishful thinking or peer pressure, or is it the voice of God, urging us forward, calling us to respond in faith? If it's the latter, then there's one more question we need not only to ask but also to answer: isn't it time to decide?

Pray

Time to decide?
Come off it, what's the rush?
There's ages yet . . .
  no hurry.

I want to live a little first,
  let my hair down and enjoy myself.
You're only young once, after all –
  time for the serious stuff later.
Time to decide?
Not yet, Lord –
  tomorrow will do.
I'm busy right now,
  no time to stop –
  come back another day.
You understand, don't you?
It's not that I don't want to listen,
  but there's the house, the garden, the job, the family –
  so much to do and so little time to do it.
I'll get round to you eventually, I promise.

Time to decide?
But I'm frightened, Lord –
  scared of what you might ask,
  what committing myself might involve.
I don't like to say no,
  but I'm terrified of saying yes,
  so give me a little longer,
  just a few more days.
Please!

Time to decide?
Do I have to?
I'm happy with the way things are,
  quite content to plod along –
  why go upsetting the apple cart?
Let's leave it for now, shall we? –
  wait until the moment's right.
You don't mind, do you?

Time to decide?
Fair enough, Lord, I'm ready.
What was that?
Too late!
The decision made.
I don't understand what you mean.
Lord, I'm listening.
I'm ready!
Lord?

47
A personal response

To all who received him and believed in his name, he gave the right to become children of God; children born not of blood or any union of the flesh, nor of any human desire, but of God.
John 1:12-13

There's nothing to touch experiencing something for ourselves. We can hear about it from others, and to a point share in it vicariously, but unless we see or share in it firsthand, then our appreciation will always be partial. The same is true in relation to the good news of Christ. It is not enough merely to hear about him from others, for faith cannot be learned, any more than it can be inherited. Rather than just knowing *about* Jesus, we need to know him personally; instead of simply *believing* in God, we need to enter into a living relationship with him through his Spirit, and go on cultivating that relationship each day, responding each moment from the heart. Have we done that? Do we still do it? The world-changing message of Christ's coming, living, dying and rising among us remains as real today as ever. Don't take my word for it – find out for yourself.

Pray

Living God,
all too easily I turn faith into knowing *about* you
rather than knowing you personally;
into a matter of outward observance
rather than inner response;
into accepting what others say concerning you
rather than rejoicing
in a firsthand experience of your love.

I forget what should concern me most:
that you want *my* response,
my love,
my commitment as much as any.
Forgive me for losing sight of that truth –
for seeing the gospel in terms of others
rather than me.
Forgive me for asking you to change the world
but keeping myself out of the equation.
Save me from a second-hand discipleship –
one that says more about what I'm meant to believe
than what I believe in my heart.
Open my eyes to your presence,
my ears to your word,
my mind to your will,
my heart to your grace
and my spirit to your renewing touch.
Teach me to see and know
that the gospel is not just good news for others
but also good news for me,
through Jesus Christ my Lord.
Amen.

48
An indifferent response

He entered the world – a world that owed its very existence to him; yet the world did not recognise him. He came to those who were his own, but his own people did not acknowledge him.
John 1:10-11

Some things don't change, do they? Just as few recognised Jesus as the Messiah when he first came, so few recognise him today. It's not that people are opposed to Christianity, rather that it fails to stir up strong feelings either way, at least outside the Church. The most common reaction – and perhaps the greatest threat – is apathy, an indifference to whatever the gospel has to say. In part this reflects the Church's failure to move with the times, in part a failure among Christians to interpret the gospel in credible terms for our modern age, and in part – perhaps the largest part – a desire to sidestep the disturbing challenge of Christ. Rather than admit to the possibility of awkward home truths, many prefer simply to look the other way. Is that true of us? We may count ourselves Christians but have only nominal faith, being largely indifferent to the claims of Christ upon our life. Before we shake our heads at the indifference of others let us ask ourselves how far Christ's presence shapes the way we live and shows itself in the people we are.

Pray

Lord,
    I stopped today,
    shocked and shaken,
    for I realised I'd barely thought of you for days,
    weeks,
    even months.

I'd gone through the motions –
attending church,
offering the occasional prayer –
but effectively I'd gone my own way,
without reference to you,
without seeking your will,
faith simply not an issue in the daily round of life.
I'd not rebelled,
nothing like that –
not set out to be disobedient,
to resist your will
or to ignore your presence –
but in a way I wish I had,
for it's worse, my mistake:
not hostility but indifference,
a sorry case of disinterest rather than rejection.
Forgive me, Lord,
for little by little I've lost touch,
neglecting my side of our relationship,
casual in discipleship,
and slowly love has grown cold,
commitment weak,
faith fractured.
Confront me again with your living word,
challenge me through the grace of Christ,
stir me by your mighty Spirit,
and so kindle the flame of trust
and the fire of love within me;
a response from the heart made new each day.
Amen.

49
An unreserved response

Peter said to Jesus, 'Why can't I follow you now, Lord? I'm ready to lay down my life for you!' 'Really?' answered Jesus. 'Is that what you think? Let me tell you this – before you hear the cock crowing you will have denied me three times.' John 13:37-38

'Tis not the dying for a faith that's difficult,' said William Makepeace Thackeray, 'tis the living up to it', and how true that is. Professing undying allegiance sounds good but doesn't actually amount to much if our words fail to back up our actions. Such was the case with Simon Peter, his bluster and bravado soon to be exposed when the chips were down. The problem, of course, was that Jesus proved to be a very different Messiah than Peter anticipated, albeit, of course, a far greater one. Just as *we* tend to, Peter wanted Jesus to fit in with his expectations, conform to his wishes, fulfil his dreams and realise his hopes. All that is perfectly understandable, but it amounts to putting ourselves into the place of God rather than giving him the place he deserves. True commitment means allowing him to work in whatever ways he wishes, putting him first and ourselves second. How far does such total trust and obedience characterise your response?

Pray

Living God,
  I thought I'd responded,
  that I'd professed my faith
  and offered my commitment,
  but I hadn't,
  not fully,
  not as you wanted me to.

I'd offered a part of me,
but the rest was still firmly mine,
ring-fenced,
not to be disturbed,
kept quietly away from any challenge you might bring.
I was ready to serve,
as long as your goals were mine;
ready to follow,
as long as our paths coincided;
but the thought of loving proving costly,
discipleship bringing demands . . .
well, quite simply I pushed it aside,
hoping that what I couldn't see I could safely ignore.
Only I couldn't,
for instead of having a foot in both camps,
I didn't have one in either,
life lived neither fully for me nor fully for you.
Forgive me, Lord,
and teach me to consecrate myself
wholly to your service:
to be used as you would use me,
to serve as you would have me serve,
confident that,
though I may not have the resources needed,
your strength will see me through.
In the name of Christ I ask it.
Amen.

50
The compelling call

The crowd, having heard Jesus out to the end, were dumbfounded at his teaching, for he spoke with an aura of natural authority, quite unlike anything they had heard from their scribes. Matthew 7:28

Some words carry a special authority, don't they? Whereas some people talk out of the back of their heads, clearly having little if any real knowledge of their subject, others speak with conviction and credibility borne of experience. We trust what they say because their words ring true – who and what they are backing up the claims they make. So it was for the multitudes drawn to Jesus. They saw in him someone whose words linked the ordinary with the heavenly, making God relevant to the humdrum routine of life. What do *you* make of him – his words and teaching, his life and death, his message and ministry? Do those speak to you of a crank or charlatan, an impostor or fanatic, or do you see rather one whose words and deeds were one, who speaks with authority to your life? Read the story again, reflect on his words with an open mind, and then ask if you can honestly say that nothing there has failed to touched you, not simply superficially but deep within. If so, isn't it time to stop wavering and to make your response?

Pray

Lord,
  there are so many voices clamouring for my attention,
  so many people telling me how to run my life –
  books and newspapers,
  radio and television,
  family and friends,

folk in the Church,
each offering words, words, words.
They mean well, no doubt –
well, most of them, anyway –
and I need what they offer,
for my knowledge is partial,
my understanding limited,
my horizons flawed.
I can't go it alone
and I wouldn't want to,
the insights of others being a vital complement to my own,
their advice, influence and guidance
a healthy balance to my errors and weaknesses,
but they can only offer signposts,
not provide the way;
at best afford glimpses of reality,
not embody truth itself;
the most any can offer being a window on to life,
rather than life in all its fullness.
Your word, Lord, is different:
simple yet profound,
disturbing yet full of promise,
revealing my emptiness yet filling to overflowing,
exposing all that is wrong within me
yet bringing inner healing.
I struggle to understand sometimes –
for so much in life troubles and confuses –
but you speak like no other,
touching the very soul,
and though I might resist,
evade,
you go on calling,
questioning,
confronting.
How can I do anything but respond?
Amen.

51
Firm foundations

Whoever hears my words and acts on them will be like someone who wisely constructed a house on an outcrop of rock. On the other hand, to hear my words and fail to apply them is akin to the fool who built his house on sand. Matthew 7:24, 26

Reading the familiar parable of Jesus concerning the wise and foolish builders, we may feel it goes without question which of the two we are most like. After all, we might say, we've put our trust in Christ, committed our lives to him in faith, so what more could possibly be needed? Well, perhaps, but is that actually what Jesus asks? Take another look at the parable and we notice that Jesus didn't say, 'Everyone who hears my words will be like a wise person who built his house on rock', but, 'Everyone who hears my words and *acts on them* . . .' The two are very different. It's not hearing the words of Jesus that matters, not even accepting they are true; what counts is whether they make a difference to who we are, whether they change the way we live. Are we still so sure we've built our house on rock?

Pray

I'm no fool, Lord, that's for sure.
I may have my faults,
  but I've built my life upon Christ,
  the chief cornerstone,
  the rock upon which all else rests.
No danger, then, of my faith falling,
  my commitment starting to crumble,
  for I've done all I need to do, surely –
  made the decision that shapes everything,
  holds all of life together.

At least that's what I thought,
until I studied your message,
truly studied it,
and suddenly I felt less sure of my ground,
for it unsettles,
troubles,
disturbs,
portraying someone else, not me:
a quality of discipleship I rarely if ever attain;
a depth of wisdom, love and dedication
that I often aspire to
yet get nowhere near.
I realise your love sets no conditions –
that salvation is down to your grace
rather than my goodness –
but you must at least hope for results,
something to show that I've changed,
that I'm serious about loving you in return –
and even if *you* can live without that,
I can't,
for if I fail to make you part of me –
putting your word into practice
and honouring your will –
then it's only a matter of time, I fear,
before I drift away,
my relationship with you
becoming more apparent than real.
So help me, Lord, truly to base my life on you;
to build each day on firm foundations,
solid rock.
It's not easy, I know that,
requiring patience, effort, determination,
but you've given me the bricks and mortar –
now help me to build!
Amen.

52
Whose will?

Father, if it is possible, spare me this cup, yet let your will be done, not mine. Luke 22:42

We like to think we know best, don't we, never mind what others tell us. So often, until we've seen and tried something for ourselves, we won't be satisfied and, in consequence, we end up learning the hard way. Our approach to life can best be summed up by that classic song immortalised by the late Frank Sinatra, 'I did it my way!' Undeniably, there are times when we need to think for ourselves and accept responsibility for our own actions, but equally there are occasions when we need the humility to listen to others. By definition, of course, that's especially true when it comes to God, he surely the one who knows what's best for us, but though we may echo the words of Jesus, 'your will be done', how often do we truly mean that? To seek God's will and follow it takes faith, humility and courage. Are we ready to take that step?

Pray

'Your will be done,
  on earth as it is in heaven.'
Yes, I know I said it, Lord,
  but I didn't expect you to take me literally;
  never imagined for a moment
  you'd hold me to the bargain.
Change the world by all means,
  others too, come to that,
  but me? –
  can't you make an exception?

What I meant by 'Your will be done',
  was '*Let* it be your will',
  not '*If* it be'.
Come on, Lord, be reasonable.
You know best, I realise that,
  and of course your purpose comes first,
  but surely you can work round me,
  fit my requests into your plan somewhere?
That's not too much to ask, is it?
You know what I want from you,
  how much it means to me –
  don't go spoiling things, please.
What's that you say?
I've got things wrong,
  my priorities, muddled.
Now hang on, Lord,
  I've said it once,
  I'll say it again,
  'Not your will but mine be done.'
Whoops, I got that wrong, didn't I?
Or did I?

SHARING OUR FAITH

53
Meaningful witness

Go and make disciples of all people. Matthew 28:19a

There are few things to beat the enthusiasm of childhood. The spontaneity of youngsters rushing out of school at the end of the day to tell their parents what they have been doing and to display their latest piece of work is something special indeed, a priceless gift to be treasured while it lasts. At such an age there is always something to share. Sadly, we lose that as the years pass. But there is one area of life where we should still have that desire to share bubbling up within us. In the Gospels we see it in all those whose lives were touched by Jesus: shepherds hurrying from the stable; lepers made clean and others healed; ordinary men and women who had found hope, peace, joy and purpose. We, of course, have not seen and heard in quite the same way, but Jesus has touched our lives nonetheless, and goes on doing so day by day. Do we see that as good news to share? Do our eyes sparkle with a child's enthusiasm to pass it on? Do we yearn to make known what we have seen and heard? God has given us good news in Christ. What are we doing to share it?

Pray

Lord Jesus Christ,
  you call me to witness to others,
  to make known what you have done for me,
  and I want to do just that:
  to tell of your gracious love
  and to share how much you mean to me,
  only I'm not sure where,
  or when,
  or how.

I don't want to preach at others,
  to force my beliefs down their throats.
I don't want to push religion,
  spouting on about faith every moment.
I want to talk naturally,
  impulsively,
  speaking of you when it is right to do so,
  testifying at the appropriate time and place,
  in a meaningful way,
  so that *my* words ring true
  and *your* word hits home.
But it's not easy, Lord,
  for I come up against so many preconceptions,
  such that the words I use are rarely what is heard.
Teach me, then, what you would have me say
  and help me to say it,
  sensitively, spontaneously and sincerely,
  to the glory of your name.
Amen.

54
A time and a place

Do not toss what is sacred to the dogs, or feed pearls to swine, for they will simply stamp all over them or turn and attack you. Matthew 7:6

What do you make of those words of Jesus? They're disturbing, aren't they, appearing to undermine everything we know and believe about him, but don't be deceived. He wasn't indulging here in spiritual snobbery or elitism, but was employing instead the common rabbinic teaching device of using language designed to shock in order to get his message home. Anyone who has ever tried to share their faith will empathise with the point he was trying to make, for they will be well aware of the frustration of sharing what seems hugely exciting only for it to be treated with disdain, of no interest whatsoever. Time and again our attempts at witnessing to Christ can meet with apathy and indifference, few if any wanting to listen. The reasons are many, and it's not for us to judge, but the thrust of Jesus' words, at least as I understand them, is that we should not persist in pushing the gospel where it is not wanted. Do that and we may end up doing more harm than good. It is God who wins people to faith, not our clever arguments. There comes a time then when, having done our best, we must leave to him what we cannot do.

Pray

I should have stopped, Lord, shouldn't I? –
realised that enough was enough.
But instead I ploughed on regardless,
convinced that I could make a difference.

I spoke because I wanted to make you known –
to share my faith and communicate your love –
but the blank eyes and wrinkled brow
should have told me to let go,
to realise that the time wasn't right,
the person not ready,
the stage not set.
I spoke again,
this time because I thought I had to,
believing it my duty to witness to you
and declare your name,
but the flashing eyes and narrowed brow
should have warned me off,
telling me that the moment was wrong,
the person hostile,
the soil infertile.
I meant well,
and was right to try,
but who knows the harm I've done,
the damage I've caused,
by outstaying my welcome,
carrying on where I wasn't wanted.
Alongside eagerness and enthusiasm, Lord,
give me sensitivity.
Alongside obedience to your word,
give me discernment.
Teach me when to speak
and when to keep silent;
what to say
and what is best left unspoken.
Teach me that there's a time and place for everything,
and help me to know when each one is.
Amen.

TEACH US TO PRAY

55
Any requests?

Ask, and you will receive; seek, and you will find what you're looking for; knock, and the door will be thrown open. Matthew 7:7

If ever the danger of taking Scripture out of context was apparent, it can surely nowhere be clearer than in the first few words of our passage today: 'Ask, and you will receive'. Many have used that statement to argue that we need only request something with sufficient faith and it will be ours. Imagine the consequences were that actually so: God would be at our beck and call, subject to whatever whim happened to take our fancy. It would make a mockery of everything we believe, for instead of looking to do *his* will we would be expecting him to do *ours.* The implications are unthinkable – a recipe for chaos and disaster. What Jesus is actually saying though is very different, the sort of request he has in mind being for spiritual enlightenment, a deeper knowledge of God, a closer relationship with him. Lobby him with a list of personal demands and there's no knowing what his response might be. Ask though for lasting treasure, search for true fulfilment, knock at the door of his kingdom, seeking to be part of it, and, make no mistake, he will delight to hear and answer.

Pray

'Help me,' I prayed.
'Take away this problem.'
'Provide those funds.'
'Grant that job.'
In these and a host of other ways, Lord,

I've come to you in prayer,
asking for first this,
then that –
as though you're a blank cheque,
a guarantee card assuring that I will secure
whatever blessing I seek.
But it's not like that, is it?
You *may* say yes, of course –
indeed, you often do –
but you may equally say no,
faith not a promise of earthly comfort
but of heavenly blessing.
You want me to ask, certainly,
to seek
and to knock at the door,
but you've made clear also
what the object of my asking should be,
the goal of my search,
the purpose of my knocking –
each concerned with your kingdom
and your righteousness;
with leading me closer to you
and teaching me more of your way,
so that I might know and serve you better.
I'll still ask as I used to, Lord,
still seek your blessing in the daily affairs of life,
for I need your guidance and help so much,
but teach me also and especially
to ask for what really matters,
to search for eternal riches,
to knock at the gates of life in all its fullness,
knowing that you will be there,
waiting to fling them open and welcome me in.
Amen.

56
Simple prayer

When praying, do not pile up empty words in the way the Gentiles do, imagining they will be heard because of their eloquence. Do not copy them, for your Father knows everything you need before you even ask him. Matthew 6:7-8

How often are we guilty in prayer of the mistake Jesus highlights in the verses above? If your prayers are anything like mine, God must sometimes feel bombarded by a barrage of words. We don't intend it to be that way, but since God doesn't physically speak, and since we also tend to have a lot on our minds, prayer tends to be hopelessly one-sided. Compare such prayers with the model Jesus set out in the Lord's Prayer, and the content could hardly be more different, for the prayer is succinct yet profound, its focus primarily on God rather than ourselves. This is not to say that words don't have their place in prayer – of course they do, and I'm sure God is delighted to listen – but we need also to make time for silence, focusing on God, recognising his greatness and seeking a greater understanding of his purpose. We need to recognise that he knows our needs and longs to meet them, and that the most faithful prayer we can therefore ever offer is just a few words long: 'Your will be done'! Next time you pray, then, spend a little less time talking and a little more reflecting; you won't be disappointed.

Pray

Was it a prayer, Lord?
It was meant to be,
    and of course it was, to a point,
    yet I came away feeling frustrated,

unsatisfied,
as though something was missing,
as though I hadn't got through.
I see it now,
your answer suddenly becoming clear:
I spoke *to* you, not *with* you,
scarcely pausing for breath to listen;
more intent on listing *my* wishes
than seeking *your* will,
with having *my* say than hearing *your* word.
You listened, no doubt –
graciously and lovingly as ever –
but you knew what I needed before I asked you,
and you knew, too, that my greatest need
was simply to spend time with you –
quietly,
reflectively,
reverently –
focusing on your goodness,
recognising your love
and rejoicing in your grace.
Teach me to do that, Lord:
to understand that prayer is more than a wish list,
a catalogue of requests.
May it instead be an encounter,
a time of meeting;
an opportunity to glimpse your purpose
and to commit myself more fully to it,
giving you always, in all things,
the praise, glory, honour and worship
that is due to you,
this day and for evermore.
Amen.

57
Self-centred prayer

Tread carefully when you enter the house of God. Better to draw near and listen than to offer the sacrifice of fools, for they cannot keep themselves from doing evil. Never be in a hurry to talk and do not let your heart speak hastily before God, for God is in heaven and you are upon earth. So, then, let your words be few. Ecclesiastes 5:1-2

What is the chief subject of our prayers? In all likelihood, the focus is on us. We don't mean to be self-centred, it just happens, our prayers all too often resembling a personal wish list. 'Grant me this,' we say, without any sense of incongruity; 'do such and such . . . help me in so and so', as if we fully expect God to be at our beck and call. Yet, of course, we claim that the one we worship is sovereign over all, ruler of heaven and earth, and Lord of space and time. If that is so, shouldn't our prayers focus as much on him as us, not just offering him praise, thanksgiving and confession, but also seeking his will rather than attempting to dictate our own? If we really believe God is who we say he is, surely the right approach in prayer has to be to listen to what he wants and to put his wishes and interests before our own.

Pray

It was a prayer, Lord,
 of sorts anyway –
 a cry from the heart expressing my need of you,
 my longing for help –
 but it was too much about me
 and too little about you.
Nothing new there, of course,
 that's the sad thing.

I wish I could say otherwise:
that I made time to praise you,
my first thought and spontaneous desire
to acknowledge your goodness
and rejoice in your love,
but it's not like that, I'm afraid,
rarely like that at all.
And as for thanksgiving,
I'm ashamed to say it all too rarely enters my head.
I pray for others, grant me that,
yet even there something's wrong,
for it's usually the select few:
family, friends, colleagues –
you know the sort of thing.
I guess my forte is confession,
I'm A1 in that department,
but even there I'm more concerned to evade judgement
than to express true remorse.
It's all about me, Lord, isn't it? –
my needs,
my hopes,
my faults,
my loved ones –
and though I know *you* don't condemn me for that,
I can't help condemning myself,
feeling that somewhere I've lost the plot,
failed to appreciate this gift you've given.
So I'm here now with one more prayer,
as much from the heart as any –
about me again, it's true,
but genuinely wanting it to be about you as well:
Lord, teach me to pray!
Amen.

58
God-centred prayer

Give us each day our daily bread. Matthew 6:11

'And this,' said the couple, showing me round their delightful cottage, 'was another answer to prayer. We asked God to provide the right place and this is what he's given.' They were evidently sincere, yet I couldn't help but question whether prayer had anything at all to do with their plush new home. Does God really provide us with the perks of life? Is that what prayer is all about? The model Jesus gives us suggests otherwise, his words 'daily bread' indicating that we should seek only what we need to get by, not what we would like but what we can't do without. Faith is not a celestial investment scheme, guaranteeing lucrative dividends in the here and now. It is rather the conviction that, whatever we face, God will sufficiently meet our needs – physical, emotional and spiritual – for us to stay true to him and to persevere in his service until our journey's end. Then, and only then, are we guaranteed his unreserved, unlimited and unending blessing.

Pray

I prayed, Lord . . .
  I waited . . .
  and nothing happened . . .
  my request not granted,
  my faith, it seemed, in vain.
And I was puzzled,
  disappointed,
  even angry,
  wondering why you'd let me down,
  why my faithfulness in prayer

and diligence in devotion
had apparently been spurned –
unanswered and unrewarded.
And then I read those words again –
'Give us today our daily bread' –
and I realised it wasn't you at fault
but me,
for I'd failed to listen or learn,
my prayer more about desires than needs,
about life's little extras
rather than the things that really matter.
It wasn't daily bread I was asking for,
but daily treats –
health, wealth and the like,
whether for me or my loved ones.
Not, of course, that there's anything wrong with those;
quite the contrary, you delight to see all creation
rejoicing in your blessings,
celebrating your countless gifts.
Yet, above all, you want me to experience
the sheer joy of knowing you,
the wonder of understanding more fully
the extent of your love
and breadth of your purpose.
Teach me, then, not to dwell on myself in prayer,
or my own small world,
but to focus on you,
recognising who you are,
what you have done
and what you have yet to do.
Help me to open my life to your living word
and transforming grace,
so that I may receive not merely daily bread
but also food for my soul,
nourishment that satisfies now and always.
Amen.

59
Unanswered prayer

Don't stay silent, God; please don't hold your peace! Listen and answer me, O Lord, for I am enduring hardship and in need. Let my prayer reach you. Bend your ear to me and hear my cry. I'm calling, Lord, please answer! Psalm 83:1; 86:1; 88:2; 102:1a; 4:1a

Prayer can be an exasperating business sometimes, can't it? We feel as though we are beating our heads against a brick wall, struggling to get through to God but getting nowhere. Even when we're confident God has heard us, we can wait sometimes in vain for an answer, until eventually we begin to question whether he was listening after all. Innumerable Christians must, at some time in their lives, have wrestled with the conundrum of unanswered prayer without coming up with satisfactory answers, and I am no different. There are times when it is simply impossible to offer convincing explanations, and all we can do is trust and wait. At other times, though – perhaps more often than we might realise – it may be that God has answered all along, only we've failed to recognise him speaking.

Pray

I prayed, Lord.
I watched and I waited,
  trusting,
  expecting,
  hoping . . .
  but nothing happened.
I prayed again,
  crying out for help,
  pleading for guidance,

and this time I was not only sure you'd answer
but also confident of what the answer would be.
Only it didn't turn out that way –
life taking an unforeseen twist,
shattering my illusions,
crushing my hopes,
and leaving faith teetering,
balanced over a precipice.
I called again,
begging you this time,
promising you undying loyalty,
total commitment,
if you would just respond to my plea . . .
but yet again the answer was wanting,
and I felt lost,
confused,
frightened;
everything that had seemed so certain
suddenly so insecure.
But then you spoke –
through the counsel of a friend,
the testimony of Scripture,
the prompting of your Spirit,
the circumstances of life –
and I realised you'd been speaking all along,
giving your reply,
except the answer was different
to the one I'd looked for,
your purpose breaking out of the fetters
I'd placed upon it,
refusing to be confined.
I'd prayed,
I'd trusted,
but I'd anticipated the wrong thing,
expecting you to act as I wanted
instead of giving myself to your will.

Forgive me, Lord,
   and teach me to open my eyes to the unexpected,
   to the constant surprise of your love.
Amen.

60
Time to pray

He persuaded his disciples to board the boat and cross to the other side ahead of him, while he dismissed the crowds. Then, having done that, he went up the mountain by himself to pray. As evening fell, he was there alone. Matthew 14:22-23

How often do you set aside time for quiet prayer and devotion? The importance of doing so is best exemplified in Jesus and the way throughout his ministry he repeatedly drew aside from the crowds to make time and space for God. Those moments of contemplation and communion were his lifeblood, nurturing the bond he enjoyed with his Father, nourishing his spirit, and giving him the strength he needed to stay true to his calling. If Jesus depended on such times, how much more do we! Yes, I know it's hard sometimes, that there are always 101 other things to do, but most of us can find a few moments if we really want to. It's a question of priorities, of what we value most in life, and if we can't find space for God, then clearly he's not as important to us as we like to believe. Whatever else you have to do, whatever other demands you're facing, ensure you spend a few moments of quiet each day to get to know a little better the one who knows you inside out. Do that, and everything else will find its time and place also.

Pray

I wondered where you were, Lord;
  why you seemed so strangely absent,
  failing to hear my prayers,
  failing to respond.
It was as though faith was divorced from life,
  day after day lived with no reference to your will
  or any sense of your guidance and purpose.

But then the truth dawned:
  it wasn't *you* who was absent
  but *me*.
You'd been there all along,
  waiting to meet me,
  to listen
  and to answer,
  present every moment of every day
  if only I would see it.
I'd rushed from one thing to another,
  scurrying here, there and everywhere
  in a bid to get things done,
  but I'd forgotten what mattered most:
  spending time,
  alone,
  with you.
I'd taken it for granted you'd be there,
  and I was right in that, at least,
  but I'd forgotten that, if I want to hear your voice
  and feel your closeness,
  I need to be there with you,
  listening,
  learning,
  giving
  and receiving,
  getting to know you as you know me.
Teach me, Lord, next time you seem distant,
  next time I wonder why you've lost touch,
  to pause
  and ponder,
  and to remember that, in all likelihood,
  you're asking the same question of me,
  only in *your* case,
  unlike mine,
  with good cause!
Amen.

61
Patient prayer

I waited patiently for the Lord to hear me, and he did so, listening to and answering my prayer. Psalm 40:1

'All things come to those who wait' says the old proverb, but is that true? Many will know from painful experience that this is not always so. We can beg God to do something, implore him day after day, and yet wait in vain, his only answer seeming to be a resounding 'No!' Occasionally that may indeed be his answer, but not necessarily. It may be that we need to be patient, the time not yet right for our request to be granted. Only time will tell. The testimony of the Psalmist, however, along with countless others in Scripture and across the years, counsels us not to give up hope, for if something accords with God's purpose, then it will ultimately be done. We need to trust his timing, recognising that it may not correspond to our own, holding firm to the conviction that, by his grace, good things come to those who wait.

Pray

What's happening, Lord?
When are you going to hear me?
You can't say I haven't been patient,
  for it's not just been months now but years –
  long frustrating years of waiting,
  longing,
  hoping –
  and still no sign of an answer.
I've kept faith –
  or at least I've tried to –

but it's not been easy,
not easy at all,
for didn't you say, 'Ask, and you will receive',
'Seek, and you will find'?
Well, I've asked,
I've sought,
and I'm still seeking,
but there's no sign of much happening,
no suggestion you're about to respond.
Lord,
help me to be patient,
to recognise that your timing is not the same as mine.
Help me to trust,
putting faith in your purpose before my own.
Teach me that you *do* hear
and you *will* answer,
but when and where is down to you,
and in that assurance may I find the strength to wait
for as long as you ask.
Amen.

TRUE FULFILMENT

62
Treasure in heaven

Do not amass earthly treasures for yourselves . . . Focus instead on treasures in heaven, vulnerable neither to moth, rust nor theft. For you can be sure of this; wherever your treasure is to be found, your heart will be found too. Matthew 6:19a, 20

You can't take it with you, we sometimes say. So it is now and so it has always been. Not, of course, that the prospect of wealth isn't an attractive one. We'd all, I'm sure, like to see a little more in our pay packets, a growth in our investments, or a windfall to tide us over in early retirement, but if we imagine that such things would guarantee contentment or promise a cure to our ills, then we're sadly mistaken. It may be a cliché to say that money doesn't buy us happiness, but it's true nonetheless: no price can be put on the gifts God offers – peace, joy, hope, love, life, fulfilment. These cannot be bought or hoarded away – they must be received with thanksgiving and shared with similar gratitude – and the wonder is that such gifts *can* be taken with us, for they extend beyond death for all eternity!

Pray

Forgive me, Lord,
  for I'd forgotten how rich I was.
I looked at others,
  and saw what they earned or owned,
  and I was jealous,
  asking why *I* shouldn't have the same,
  and, before I knew it,
  instead of appreciating what I had
  I found myself dwelling on all I didn't have,
  wanting more of this,

more of that,
more of everything.
Yet whatever I acquired, I coveted something extra,
possessions failing to satisfy as I'd expected,
pleasing enough for a moment,
but their shine soon fading.
I'd lost sight, Lord, of what's truly of value:
joy,
peace,
hope,
love;
the knowledge that I'm valued by you,
accepted for what I am;
the assurance of your forgiveness;
the daily experience of your presence,
by my side
and deep within.
There's no price I can put on those,
for their worth is beyond measure,
too wonderful for words,
yet you offer them freely,
not just now but for all eternity.
Save me, then, from chasing after illusory happiness,
from attempting to fill my life
with what can never truly fulfil.
Teach me simply to look to you
and to open my heart to your grace,
recognising that you have blessed me in abundance –
that I am rich indeed.
Amen.

63
Truly satisfied

Blessed are those who are hungry and thirsty for righteousness; they will be satisfied. Matthew 5:6

Few of us have any real idea what hunger is, either physically or spiritually. We may have experienced a rumbling stomach from time to time, even perhaps have missed the occasional meal or fasted for a day, but when one compares that with the starving millions of our world, it quickly pales into insignificance. To crave not so much our next meal but simply a morsel to eat is simply not part of our experience, yet that's the sort of hunger God wants us to show for spiritual things: a deep, urgent yearning to know more of him and to serve him better. Sadly we tend to hunger instead for other things – money, possessions and the like – cramming ourselves with so much that is insubstantial, unable ultimately truly to satisfy. The result, of course, is spiritual emaciation, stunted growth as Christians, and a gnawing emptiness deep within.

Pray

Lord,
    I don't know what it is to be hungry . . .
    really hungry . . .
    for I'm one of the world's lucky ones,
    having more than enough food to eat every day.
The most I get is peckish,
    relishing the thought of a good meal,
    but that's enough for me to recognise
    that I rarely hunger either for spiritual things,
    let alone thirst after righteousness.

I may have done once,
yearning for something to give shape
and direction to my life,
and perhaps in the early days,
the first flush of commitment,
I *was* eager,
devouring your word expectantly,
aching to feast more deeply
in times of prayer and worship.
But that's all a memory now,
a dim recollection,
the reality today so very different.
Far from craving nourishment
I take the occasional snack,
the odd nibble,
the isolated sip,
feeding on your word as the inclination takes me,
dipping into desultory acts of devotion,
snatching a quick dose of prayer in times of crisis . . .
and that's about it.
No wonder I struggle, Lord,
my faith fragile,
my discipleship weak,
for that's no kind of diet,
hardly enough even to sustain life,
let alone encourage growth.
Forgive me,
and create in me, through your Spirit,
a genuine and passionate desire
for the things of your kingdom:
a hankering truly to love you,
a longing to contribute more fully
to the work of your kingdom,
an unquenchable appetite to reach maturity in Christ.
I've not been hungry, Lord,
nor thirsted as I should,

but at least now I see it
and realise how empty I am.
Come, then,
keep hunger alive,
and, in your mercy, satisfy me,
body and soul,
day by day.
Amen.

64
Real peace

Peace is my bequest to you – my own peace, unlike anything the world can give. So, then, do not be anxious or fearful in heart.
John 14:27

Mention peace and people will think of different things: peace of mind, inner serenity, a place of tranquillity, the absence of war, or even simply the absence of noise. Which of these corresponds to the peace Jesus talks of? The answer, of course, is none, this peace being unlike any other, but the first two of those options can at least point to what he had in mind, for the gift he offers is an all-pervading serenity of spirit arising from an assurance of God's love in all circumstances – an inner stillness, in other words, that is somehow able to endure even in times of turmoil. It is a peace that has sustained people across the ages, a peace that truly passes all understanding. Words cannot suffice to express this most precious of gifts, but words are not needed. It is open to all, offered freely, lovingly and constantly in Christ, the King of kings and Lord of lords – the Prince of Peace.

Pray

I looked for peace, Lord,
  but I didn't find it.
I looked at the world,
  but I saw there division and discord –
  person divided against person
  and nation against nation;
  hatred, greed and bitterness
  exploding into violence and war.

I looked at myself,
  but I saw there a restless striving for contentment,
  an outward calm masking an inner turmoil.
I looked at the Church,
  and even there the wounds ran deep,
  conflict over worship and doctrine,
  clashes of temperament and personality,
  petty disputes dividing Christian from Christian,
  fellowship from fellowship,
  estranging us from you and one another.
I looked for peace, Lord,
  and I didn't find it,
  until I looked to you,
  and then I found rest for my soul,
  a haven from the storm,
  a quietness deep within.
Amen.

TRUST IN GOD'S FUTURE

See also FAITH AND DOUBT

65
Trust in God's promises

I have spoken, and I will make it happen; I have planned, and I will accomplish it. Isaiah 46:11b

We live today in an age when promises are two a penny, made today and broken tomorrow. Politicians, for example, promise to increase spending on such and such, to tackle this, achieve that. But do they? Well, sometimes maybe, but all too often such pledges are exposed as empty rhetoric, political posturing designed simply to woo voters prior to an election. What, then, of the promises of Scripture: how far can we trust them? Is it true that where two or three gather in the name of Christ, he will be there in the midst of them? Is it true that he will be with us always, to the end of time? Is it true that whoever believes in him will not die but will instead inherit eternal life? Is it true that nothing can ever separate us from the love of God, which is ours through Jesus Christ our Lord? The triumphant message of Scripture is that not only these but also all the promises God has given are true, and if we doubt that we need only look to Christ, the fulfilment of so many hopes, the realisation of so many promises of old. Everything God has committed himself to do, he *will* do. Whatever he has said should happen, *will* happen. In a world of broken promises, that's one pledge we can stake our life on.

Pray

Eternal God,
  I *say* I believe in your promises,
  but sometimes I'm not as sure as I'd like to be.

When it comes to stepping out in faith,
taking risks for your kingdom;
to receiving mercy,
and accepting I'm truly forgiven;
to death and resurrection,
holding firm to the assurance you have given
of life beyond the grave,
I *do* believe,
but my trust is fragile,
threatened by doubts and questions,
at risk of being broken.
Remind me of all you have already done across the years,
the promises you have so wonderfully honoured
and prophecies so gloriously fulfilled.
Remind me of the words
I personally have found to be true
and of the faithfulness
that so many have experienced first-hand.
So may I put my hand in yours
and hold on to you more firmly,
assured deep in my heart that your word is true,
your love constant
and your promises sure.
In Christ's name, I ask it.
Amen.

66
Prepared for anything

God is our sanctuary and protection, a constant help in times of peril. So we will fear nothing, even if this world should be turned upside down and the mountains crumble into the depths of the ocean – even if the waters of the sea thunder and churn and the mountains quiver amidst the turmoil. Psalm 46:1-3

What will tomorrow bring? We have no way of knowing, have we? Any day or moment may unexpectedly bring joy or sorrow, pleasure or pain, health or sickness, life or death – and, no matter how strong our faith, that's not an easy thought to live with. Few of us will feel confident of coping if and when life brings tragedy or disaster. Fortunately, however, it's not solely down to us. We have the assurance of God himself that his strength will be sufficient for all our needs, that nothing will ever be able to separate us from his love. If the Psalmist could write millennia ago of his confidence in God's help, how much more should we, with our experience and knowledge of Christ, be able to say the same? Not that we are in any way immune to suffering or disaster – there is no promise of that – but God promises to support us through whatever life might throw at us. Though *our* strength may fail, we can be sure that his never will.

Pray

I shouldn't be scared Lord, I know that,
  but I can't help it sometimes.
When I look at the traumas some endure –
  the anguish of body, mind and spirit –
  I can't help wondering how I'd cope in their shoes,
  whether I'd hold on, not simply to my faith,
  but also to my sanity.

Should disaster strike, would I be brave,
  resilient in time of crisis?
I'd like to think so,
  but I doubt it somehow,
  a sense of panic welling up inside me
  even at the thought,
  never mind the real thing.
Lord, strengthen me.
Teach me that, whatever may come, you will be there;
  that, however fierce the storm,
  you will bring your peace.
Teach me to surrender my fear into your hands
  and to entrust myself into your care,
  secure in the assurance that,
  no matter what life or death may bring,
  your purpose will continue
  and your love remain sure.
In Christ's name I pray.
Amen.

67
The power and the glory

For the kingdom, the power and the glory are yours, now and for evermore. Amen. Matthew 6:13b; added in some ancient manuscripts only

To me, the idea of saying the Lord's Prayer without concluding, in some form or another, with the line above is unthinkable; the words are part of the prayer I've been brought up with from childhood. Strangely, however, they don't appear in several early manuscripts of Matthew's Gospel. Did Jesus not include them? Who can say? Whatever the case, some scribes who copied out Matthew's Gospel clearly felt that the prayer was incomplete without them, so they added them on. Why did they think them important? Because, I think, the line sets the context not just for this prayer but for the whole of Jesus' life and ministry. It reminds us that though God's will is repeatedly frustrated, his kingdom not yet realised, and evil often apparently victorious, the future is secure, for all things are ultimately in his hands. Most important of all, it reminds us that this goes for us too. However much we fail, however weak our faith, however far from him we may stray, his love and purpose continues. The kingdom, power and glory are his; so also, thank God, are we.

Pray

Lord,
  I feel overwhelmed sometimes,
  dwarfed by the problems that confront this world,
  by the forces of evil we're up against,
  by the trials and tragedies of so many,
  and by the things you ask and expect of me
  in response.

These consume my attention,
 rearing up at me, daunting and forbidding,
 destroying all hope of things changing,
 least of all me.
I dwell on failure instead of success,
 defeat instead of victory,
 appalled by the scale of the obstacles
 that frustrate your will,
 rather than amazed by the resources you offer
 to overcome them
 and by the way you have so consistently worked
 over the years –
 bringing joy out of sorrow,
 hope out of despair,
 light out of darkness
 and life out of death.
Remind me again of who and what you are,
 of the great deeds you have done,
 of the promises you have given,
 of the things you are doing here and now.
Remind me that yours is the kingdom,
 the power and the glory;
 that you are the source of all that is
 and the arbiter of all that shall be;
 the Lord of heaven and earth,
 sovereign,
 exalted,
 enthroned in splendour and might.
Above all, remind me
 that what I cannot begin to achieve,
 you can accomplish
 beyond anything I might ever ask or imagine,
 and so may the only thing to overwhelm me
 as I go through life
 be a sense of your unfailing love,
 your great mercy,

your awesome power
and your gracious purpose,
through which all things
will find their fulfilment in you.
Amen.

68
A Father's love

Instead, when you pray, use words like these: Our Father in heaven . . . Matthew 6:9a

'Our Father' – we're so used to thinking of God in such terms that we scarcely give it another thought, but for the disciples, hearing Jesus use this form of address for the first time, it was revolutionary stuff: at once shocking and sensational, frightening and thrilling. They had been raised with the Old Testament idea of God as one whom nobody could look upon and live, one enthroned over all – holy, righteous, sovereign. Could it really be possible to enter into a personal relationship with him, to consider him as a father and oneself as his child? The answer brought by Jesus is an emphatic 'Yes!' Like a doting parent, God delights in our presence and longs to bless us; to do all he can, despite everything that conspires against him, to ensure our welfare, our peace of mind, security and happiness. That, says Jesus, is how he feels about us, and that is the confidence in which he wants and expects us to respond, seeing him not as some distant and dour deity – stern, strict, severe – but as one who values each of us infinitely as his children and who calls himself, simply yet wonderfully, 'our Father'.

Pray

Lord,
I need a sense of your strength:
your sovereign power,
able to move mountains and change lives,
fashioning the very universe we inhabit,
constantly at work to fulfil your purpose –

the beginning and end of all.
I need a sense of your holiness:
your passion for all that is good and true,
pure and lovely,
and your sorrow over everything
that demeans your creation
and frustrates your purpose,
separating person from person
and all from you.
I need a sense of your otherness:
your utter transcendence before which I can only kneel
in reverence and wonder,
homage and humility,
offering my heartfelt praise and worship,
for you are beyond words,
beyond comparison,
defying definition.
I need all that, Lord,
and I thank you for it,
but I need also, and especially,
to recognise you as a God of love:
the one who nurtures me like a little child;
who cherishes,
strengthens,
comforts,
teaches,
heals,
helps
and holds –
quite simply, my Father.
Amen.

69
Keeping faith

The kingdom of God is comparable to having scattered seed on the ground. Those who sow it sleep and wake night and day, and the seed sprouts and grows, though they have no idea how. The earth brings forth a crop by itself, first a shoot, then the head, then the full ear of grain. When, though, the grain is ripe, they set to work at once with their sickles, because the time for harvest has come. Mark 4:26-29

Most of us would like to think the world can be a better place, but, as the years pass, our confidence can take a battering. The harsh realities of life seem to contradict the idealistic dreams of youth, so that the first flush of faith fades to a mere shadow of what it used to be. As another natural catastrophe strikes, another country is plunged into violent conflict, another friend dies of cancer, or another person is raped, mugged or murdered, it is hard to reconcile the harsh realities of life with the picture of a loving and merciful Father. The fact that society as a whole generally dismisses any talk of God makes it all the harder to keep on believing, harder still to withstand the drip-drip effect of scorn and scepticism or sheer disinterest. Yet, as so many of the parables of Jesus remind us, if we only have eyes to see, the signs of the kingdom are all around us. Its coming is not confined to the distant future, for, in a real sense, it is also here already, the miracle of changed lives taking place every day and every moment. God is at work in a multitude of ways, prompting, encouraging, guiding, sustaining – working despite all that opposes his will to make known his love and grant his blessing. If we cannot see signs of that kingdom among us, then perhaps we are looking in the wrong place or for the wrong things!

Pray

I lose faith sometimes, Lord –
I don't mind admitting it.
When I look around me,
and see the mess I make of my life,
the mess we make of the Church
and the mess we make of our world,
I can't help feeling that it's hopeless,
any suggestion things might change for the better
simply pie in the sky,
cloud-cuckoo land.
For all my good intentions and bold resolutions,
I'm still much the same person I've always been.
For all the rhetoric of politicians,
musings of philosophers,
efforts of activists
and advances of science,
the world seems little better than in years gone by;
if anything, slightly worse.
What reason to think things can be different?
What grounds do I have for hope?
Only then I come back to you –
to your power shown on the cross:
renewing and redeeming,
bringing hope out of despair,
joy out of sorrow,
and life out of death –
power that has changed lives across the centuries
and that goes on changing them today.
I still lose faith sometimes –
I can't help it,
for I inevitably look at life with my eyes rather than yours,
but when I start to do that, Lord,
remind me again of who you are,
what you've done
and what you are still doing.

Remind me that you are greater
than the mind can conceive,
sovereign over all,
mighty beyond words –
and so may I trust in your power,
working within me and all,
able to accomplish more than I can ever ask
or begin to imagine,
to the glory of your name.
Amen.

70
Promise for the future

No eye has seen, nor ear heard, nor any heart conceived of the things that God has prepared for those who love him.
1 Corinthians 2:9

Any language we use to talk of the things of God, as with talk concerning God himself, is necessarily flawed, since we are attempting to describe the indescribable, to put into finite concepts realities that finally go beyond this world. I've tried many times to get my head round the idea of eternity. I've struggled to explain the idea of heaven to my children when they've talked to me about death. I've debated with other Christians what sort of place it might be and what kind of life we might live there, but each time I have eventually had to admit defeat. Why? Quite simply because as Christians we look forward to a kingdom and a blessing that is better than anything we can ever ask or imagine, inexpressible, beyond words. I wish I knew more, I wish I could say more, but if I attempted to do so I'd inevitably be talking about human things rather than the things of God. And with the things of God – frustratingly, teasingly, but wonderfully – there's no other option, sometimes, but to depend on faith.

Pray

Loving God,
  I try to picture what heaven is like,
  but words fail me.
I try to imagine a world of everlasting bliss,
  but it defies my limited reach of mind.
I try to comprehend the wonder of your presence,

but it is beyond me.
I try to envisage the blessings you hold in store,
but I barely know where to start.
Teach me,
though I cannot fully understand,
to continue trusting in your purpose,
looking forward in eager anticipation
to the dawn of your kingdom.
Teach me, above all,
to keep the vision alive,
confident that,
however wonderful I may glimpse your kingdom to be,
however rich in blessing and brimming over with joy,
the reality you hold in store is more special,
more breathtaking,
than anything I can ever ask
or hope for –
a treasure beyond price.
Amen.

71
Signs of his faithfulness

See how the wild flowers grow, pay heed to them. They do not labour or weave, yet I can assure you that not even Solomon in all his grandeur was decked out like one of these. If God clothes the grass of the field like this – grass that, though here today, tomorrow will be tossed on to a bonfire – will he not clothe you all the more richly, you of such little faith? Matthew 6:28b-30

Does the natural world speak unequivocally about God? Some seem to believe so, but personally I'm not convinced, for alongside its beauty and wonder there's an ugly side too; much that speaks of the forces of chaos and confusion rather than of order and a loving purpose. Yet, to the eye of faith, there is enough around us, even in things as simple as a flower bursting into bloom or a bird pecking at seed, to speak of the one who lies behind it all; the hand of God that not only fashioned the universe but that also reaches out afresh each day providing the essentials of life and the promise of life to come. Despite all that spoils and destroys, denies and disfigures, we can catch sight around us of an architect's design, a Creator's power and a sovereign purpose.

Pray

It's easy to romanticise, Lord,
  to gush about all things bright and beautiful,
  all creatures great and small,
  as though anyone need only look at these,
  and, if they have any sense whatsoever,
  they will bow down in worship,
  fall to their knees in adoration,

acknowledging you as the living God,
Creator of all.
But it's not that simple,
for alongside the good there's the bad,
beside the lovely, the ugly –
all manner of pain and suffering hidden from view –
and though some of that may be down to us,
to human ignorance, wilfulness or folly,
most is out of our hands,
impossible to control,
harder still to understand.
Yet if much confuses,
much also inspires.
If much confounds,
much also illuminates.
And if much conceals,
much also speaks of your hand at work,
your creative purpose,
your intricate design.
Lord, I know that all creation groans together,
eagerly awaiting its redemption in Christ –
that it is imperfect and incomplete –
but I thank you for those things
that nevertheless speak to me of you,
stirring the spirit,
touching the heart
and reinforcing faith that your love
will ultimately perfect all things,
leading them to their fulfilment in you.
Open my eyes more fully
to whatever may help me glimpse you better,
so that trust may grow
and faith be deepened.
In Christ's name I pray.
Amen.

UNASSUMING DISCIPLESHIP

72
True humility

Blessed are those who are poor in spirit; to them belongs the kingdom of heaven. Matthew 5:3

There can surely be few more painful experiences than to have nothing and be totally dependent on the charity of others. Yet in terms of our relationship with God we are all in precisely that position, if we did but know it. None of us deserves his goodness; no one can earn his blessing or merit his love. We come before God spiritually bankrupt, reliant upon his generosity, his willingness to give and go on giving despite rather than because of our efforts. To be poor in spirit means to recognise that total dependence on God and to open our lives to whatever he would do in them. For most of us it is an elusive quality – one that we strive to cultivate with little success. Not that this should surprise us: by definition, we depend on God for *this* gift, like any other.

Pray

Me?
Poor in spirit?
I'd like to think so, Lord,
  but I'm not, am I? –
  not by a long chalk.
Poor in faith, perhaps,
  in commitment,
  worship,
  service;
  but in terms of spirit it's an altogether different story.
I'm full of myself, truth be told,
  not in the sense of pride –
  or at least I hope not –

but in the sense of self-will,
self-centredness,
self-indulgence,
constantly putting my interests before yours,
my goals,
my dreams,
my wishes
before *your* purpose.
It's human, of course –
you know that as much as any –
but though you continue to reach out regardless,
arms outstretched in love,
I unwittingly rebuff your embrace,
turning aside,
backing away,
forever keeping you at a distance.
Forgive me, Lord,
and help me to change.
Teach me to value myself, as you do,
but above all to value you
and the things of your kingdom.
Teach me to stand tall as your child,
but also to humble myself under your mighty hand,
and so, in my need may I find succour,
and, in my poverty, riches beyond measure.
Amen.

73
A supporting role

Give my greetings to Mary, who laboured so hard on your behalf. Greet Urbanus, our fellow-worker in Christ, and my beloved friend Stachys. Greet Apelles, who has proven himself in Christ. Greet Tryphena and Tryphosa, those women who have also worked so hard in the Lord. Greet my dear friend Persis, who has toiled in so much for the Lord's sake. Greet Rufus, chosen in the Lord, and his mother, who has been a mother to me, too. Greet Asyncritus, Phlegon, Hermas, Patrobas, Hermes and the brothers with them. Greet Philologus, Julia, Nereus and his sister, and Olympas and all the saints with them. Romans 16:6, 9-10a, 12-15

What do you make of the long list of names at the end of Paul's letter to the Romans? Does it have anything to teach us, or is it simply an irrelevant aside to all but Church historians? To answer that, think for a moment of the credits at the end of a film or television programme? The only names that probably interest us are those of the cast, yet those credits remind us that infinitely more people are involved in a production than simply the people who appear on screen. Producer, director, camera-crew, musicians, make-up department, lighting technicians and numerous others – all play a part in perfecting the finished article. Similarly, many more people than we are aware of played a part in the ministry of the Apostle Paul. They were Paul's backroom staff – those who encouraged, supported, nurtured or worked alongside him behind the scenes. All right, so they may not have gone down in history as spiritual giants, yet their contribution was nonetheless vital, for without their unsung involvement Paul couldn't have functioned as he did. We do well to remember that today, for it's all too easy to overlook those who work in the background, performing unglamorous but essential tasks such as cleaning, catering, cooking, washing-up, preparing the minutes, arranging flowers and so on. Don't forget the work they do. Don't forget both to appreciate it and to show your appreciation. And if you are one of the tireless legion working away behind the scenes, don't underrate the contribution you make, even if others sometimes appear to do so. We all have gifts and roles – let's remember to value them all.

Pray

I don't mind taking a back seat, Lord,
 I really don't,
 for I'm not one to hog the limelight,
 thrust myself forward.
I'm happy with a bit part in the supporting cast,
 never comfortable on centre stage.
But a spot of recognition wouldn't come amiss;
 nothing fancy,
 just the occasional word of appreciation,
 or gesture of thanks –
 enough to let me know that someone, somewhere,
 understands what I do
 and why I do it.
Yet, small though that seems,
 it's too much, isn't it? –
 for it's still about me rather than you,
 my ego rather than your glory.
Forgive me, Lord,
 and teach me to be ready to serve you
 with no thought of reward
 and no concern for self,
 ready to be overlooked,
 taken for granted,
 even put upon for your sake.

Use me as you will,
  no matter how humble my role might be,
  so that I might further your kingdom
  and contribute to your purpose.
Amen.

74
Meek, not weak

Blessed are the meek; the earth is their inheritance.
Matthew 5:5

'Gentle Jesus, meek and mild' – for many that sums up their idea of Jesus and Christians, and it's definitely not an idea they want to be associated with. I can't blame them, for who would! If discipleship means being taken advantage of, treated like a doormat, enduring whatever is thrown at us with barely a whimper, then no thank you. But that's not at all what we see in Jesus. In him, rather, we see someone in control of his own destiny, willingly walking the way of the cross, exhibiting courage and determination that most of us can only dream of. His meekness lay solely in his total obedience and commitment to God. There is nothing weak or timid about such meekness – indeed, we may fairly ask if any of us has what it takes to display such a quality, for it may frequently be costly and demanding, asking more of us than we feel able to give. Yet if we are ready to honour God's will, he will honour us in turn, giving us the strength to do whatever he asks of us.

Pray

Lord,
save me from meekness as the world sees it:
from a spirit of timidity and indecision,
an attitude of compliance and cowardice,
a character perceived as spineless,
submissive,
subservient.

Grant me, instead, true meekness:
a willingness to trust in your purpose
and obey your commands,
to respond to your guidance and step out in faith.
Isn't that what discipleship should mean:
being ready to speak out against wrong
and stand up against evil,
to take on a challenge and venture into the unknown,
meeting obstacles, difficulties and disappointments,
yet, if it is your will,
persevering to the end,
risking all if necessary?
I don't want to be a caricature, Lord,
the sort of person who confirms the view
most people have of Christians and the Church,
and I don't believe *you* want that either.
So my prayer today is simply this:
grant me meekness,
not weakness!
Amen.

75
Down-to-earth discipleship

Think twice before making a public show of religious devotion aimed at impressing others; you will deny yourselves any reward from your heavenly Father. Matthew 6:1

We all like to show ourselves off in the best light, don't we – to be thought well of by others, admired, respected – and probably few of us can resist the temptation to make sure people are aware of our good deeds, even if it's only through the odd aside dropped casually into a conversation. Is there anything wrong with that? Probably not, as long as we avoid it becoming the overriding motive for any service we may offer, generosity show, compassion exhibit or kindnesses share. If that happens, then the deed is immediately devalued, for it becomes about us rather than others, another way of serving self rather than God. Furthermore, instead of being an expression of love, it becomes patronising and hollow, no longer sincere but a means to an end. Don't parade your virtue, says Jesus, nor seek any kind of recognition for the good you might do. Don't give for what you can get out of it, but simply for the sheer joy of giving back to the God who has given you so much.

Pray

Lord,
  I don't make a great show of prayer;
  quite the contrary,
  I far too rarely pray at all,
  days passing sometimes
  in which I forget you completely.

I don't trumpet my worship either,
instead tending to conceal it from others,
almost embarrassed, in some circles, to admit to faith
or speak of commitment.
So there's no danger, in that sense anyway,
of parading my piety on the street corner,
of holding up my virtue for all to see.
Too often the problem's the opposite:
my devotions so sporadic
that people might miss them altogether,
and my prayer-life so weak
that I couldn't crow about it
even if I wanted to.
Yet I do sometimes preen myself in public, nonetheless,
carefully ensuring, through a word here,
a comment there,
that any good I've done,
any generous word or deed,
is duly noted and applauded.
I want someone, somewhere, to say, 'Well done',
and to offer a pat on the back,
a few words of praise –
nothing fancy or over the top,
but just enough to show
that my actions haven't passed unnoticed.
Forgive me, Lord,
for even when I think I'm serving you
I'm so often serving self,
more eager to promote my name
than bring honour to yours.
Teach me to give for the joy of giving,
to love for the pleasure of loving
and to serve you for the privilege of serving,
letting that be reward enough.
Amen.